THE HEART

OF THE BHAGAVADGITA

MAHABHAGAVAT

This work is dedicated to Adi Guru Shankaracharya.

1st Reprint Edition: August 2019

Revised Reprint Edition: September 2024

This is a reprint edition of the book originally written by Saint Mahabhagavat to address the relevance of the Bhagavadgita in modern context. Content of this book is prepared on the basis of "The Heart of The Bhagavadgita originally written by Pandit Lingesh Mahabhagavat of Kurtkoti, Ph.D (His Holiness Sri Vidya Shankar Bharati Swami , Jagadguru Shankaracharya of Karvir and Sankeshwar)

The content is edited to incorporate needful corrections duly recommended by experts from the faculty of Philosophy. Another background material is also collected from Madras based publishing houses to verify different Sanskrit texts of the original volume. Utmost care is taken up to retain the normal structure of the book which was represented during its first edition.

Editor of this reprint edition is a Research Scholar of Comparative Religion and Philosophy and is working in the field of Development studies since 1995 onwards. Editor is also working in the field of Information and Communication Technology. This reprint edition is prepared in different formats (E Book, Paperback and Hard Bound).

Other publications:

Talks on the Bhagavadgita

Bhagavadgita in Daily Life

Source: Chandan Sukumar Sengupta

Arabinda Nagar, Bankura - 722101 (WB)

Contents

Foreword

The appearance of this work from the pen of His Holiness, though written no doubt before his elevation to his present high and venerable position, in a language spoken of, by those whose mother tongue it is , as the *lingua france* of India, but by contemptuous term Hoona bhasha by the so –called orthodox, is indeed a very notable sign of the time. It augurs most happily for the future well – being of the motherland, as showing the extremely liberal spirit which is coming to permeate even those high personages, who preside over the few well-known centres of religion called *Shankaracharya Peethas*, from now, a Swami, who was one of such heads enjoying the highest reverence at the hands of the thousands and thousands of his followers, mostly in this Presidency, went the length of warning a friend of mine that any one who used English translations of Hindu scripture, the Upanishads etc,. For the purpose of his study, was a patita or a fallen man, by reason of his resorting to books written on such subjects in other than Sanskrit, the sacred language. In the light of this incident, I am sure all children of Aryavarta will agree in thinking that the fact that one now occupying a similar position in the hierarchy of Hindu religious teachers and guides at the present day, has consented to the publication now of a treatise written by him, though sometimes back, in the foreign tongue of the Westerners, on the greatest of Indian scriptures, the Bhagavad Geeta, marks a transition that cannot but conduce to the growth of true spirituality in the land. For, it will lead, among other things, to the recognition of the brotherhood of all men, including the forty million and more of the so-called untouchables as the self-righteous castes and classes have been prone to characterize those brethren of theirs. That this view is not a piece of my imagination will be admitted if it is remembered that it was His Holiness who inspired the really remarkable movement which culminated in the All India Anti- Untouchability Conference, held in Bombay in March last, and by his exhortations and sympathetic letter from Delhi where he was at that time conferred on it a prestige and value that would otherwise not belong to the movement. Again, the bold appeal, made by His Holiness at a Home Rule meeting in Allahabad in a previous month as to the duty of religious heads to come forward and work for the betterment of the people in social and civic activities also, unmistakably points to the great change now taking place in those quarters which cannot but act profoundly on the national movement so manifest at present.

Before leaving this preliminary matter, it may be worth calling attention to an interesting article in one of the numbers of Samskrit journal *Vidyodaya* for 1897, brought to my notice by Pandit K. T. Srinivasachariar, the able editor of the *Suddha Dharma Mandala Series,* wherein, the bigotry of those who condemn writing in English on religious subjects. He opines that that language, instead of being derided, should be respected as *Maha Bhasha* – great language- in that it is the tongue of our rulers. He further argues for cogent reasons stated by him that, in the present circumstances of the country, there is great necessity for making our sacred books accessible to English readers by translations and otherwise. It may be added in support of the learned writer's argument that experience clearly established the capability of this Western tongue to convey more or less adequately even the subtlest ideas of Samskrit philosophical and other technical terms. It stands to reason that the tongue, which the virile race of our rulers employs for manifold purposes, must and does possess a power that is great and which is getting enriched day by day as the result of the varied activities of that race all the world over.

Turning to the treatise on hand, it is scarcely necessary to say that it would be presumption on my part to enter into any criticism of the views propounded in it, even were I at all competent to undertake such a task which is not the case. I may however be permitted to remark that those views, propounded with brevity and extreme clarity, deserve the earnest attention of every student of the Geeta.

Among those views, one requires special notice, viz., that founded on the conjunction of the phrase *Yoga* with such others as *Sankhya, Bhakti* and *Karma* so prominent in the scripture. Here, His Holiness touches upon what is cardinal in the Geeta, as will be seen from the edition thereof brought out by Pandit K. T. Srinivasachariar as No, 3 of the *Suddha Dharma Mandala* Series. The arrangement of the scripture in that edition is essentially different from the one now in general use and which latter forms the basis for His Holiness's present work. According to the former, the whole scripture, excluding certain preliminary and concluding verses, is divided into four parts, each consisting of six chapters. This division rests upon the solid foundation of the ultimate analysis of human consciousness. That consciousness, so analysed, stands, as is well known, thus: (1) *Jnana ,* *(2) Ichchha, (3) Kriya.* The first may be rendered the cognizing faculty of the Self in man or cognition; the second as the Self's faculty of desire or wish latter word apparently is derived from the same root as Ichchha; and the third as the Self's faculty of externalising and giving effect to the other two faculties by acting upon the Not-Self or matter. The synthesis of the three constitutes that for which no better English word than consciousness is as yet forthcoming; though, having regard to what Sir John Woodroffe observes, in his recent work "Shakti and Shakta" (p. 53 *et seq*) in reference to the cognate term *chit,* consciousness is hardly a satisfactory equivalent. Now, of course, neither *Jnana nor Ichchha nor Kriya* should be looked on as separate component parts capable of being tied up in water – tight compartments. They are but different aspects, each with a dominant note, of the one indivisible whole, namely, consciousness. Again, those three aspects are but reflections, in man, of the Divine attributes *chit, ananda and sat* respectively, which in common use are referred to in a different order for obvious reasons, unnecessary to explain here. Coming back to the Suddha Dharma Mandala edition, the quadruple division referred to follows the said order and consequently the four sections are known as the *Jnana, Ichchha, Kriya* and the *Samahara* or *Yoga Shastras* respectively. That this and this alone is in the fullest accord with the whole end and aim of the scripture it is impossible to doubt. For, this scripture is par excellence Yoga Shastra from the beginning to the end. No wonder therefore that in rearranging the work and making 18 chapters out of it, he, who introduced this method, found it necessary to coin such compounds as *Sankhya Yoga, Bhakti Yoga, Karma Yoga* and the rest. There can be no question that the division into three *Shatkas* was later in time than the one of four divisions. Each has its appropriate reason as *Gobhila,* the author of a most remarkable *Kartika* on the *Mahabharata,* conclusively shown in the extract from his said work quoted by me in the footnote of my Foreword to the Suddha Dharma Mandala edition referred above.

Were I to add nothing too what I have said so far, I feel I would not be expressing sufficiently my sense of the favour, shown to me in asking to write this foreword. In order to discharge more fully my obligation in the matter, I avail myself of this opportunity to offer some observations from a point of view, not perhaps the least , the Geeta admits of being regarded from.

In taking such a point of view of this scripture for consideration, I am prompted solely by the feeling that if this aspect of it comes to be altogether ignored by any considerable body of students, the loss to the thinking world in general and to the mystic world in particular will be great. One more word by way of preface to what I shall presently say. And it is that in the course of what follows, I make certain assumptions as to the goal of human progress; as to the possible developments of human faculties and powers; and as to the existence of spiritual teachers possessed of superhuman wisdom and knowledge. All this may seem incredible to some and perhaps even to many and I may thereby expose myself at their hands to the criticism that I am in regard to those assumptions a victim to unwarranted beliefs, to put it mildly. This is however inevitable in dealing with an ancient sacred book which avowedly[1] devotes itself to the exposition of how to realize Brahman, that One Changeless Reality, from which, as the Upanishads say, mind and speech return unable to attain to it. All the more so, if my present task is to be performed without detracting in any way from the reverence due to the scripture dealing with the highest theme that can occupy one's attention and in tune with the absolutely spiritual tone which pervades every line of it, expounding as it does the science described in one of its verses as the kingly science, most pure, righteous, easy to follow, capable of leading to direct experience, and productive of imperishable results. These words are no doubt scoffed at by the unfortunate materialist as an empty boast; but they are words that bring hope and joy to the man of faith, humility and intuition, the value of which last faculty is now being dinned into the ear of the west by some of her own great sons, Bergson, for example.

Now taking up the point of view to be considered, it is that the Geeta is an occult work or writing. By the term occult writing is to be understood, of course, that it contains, hidden in it as it were, ideas and truths, the comprehension of which is just in proportion to the awakening of the spiritual vision of the readers. Of the beginning of such awakening, the one unmistakable evidence will consist of the unreserved recognition of the unity of life in the infinite variety of forms in everything and everywhere, in minerals, vegetables, animals, men, devas and in the endless higher and higher states of existence throughout the cosmos, visible or invisible. I should not fail here to add the view that the Geeta is an occult scripture is expressly testified to by two words which will be found in the verse cited a little above, namely "*Raja Guhyam* – Royal secret" following "Raja –vidya" with which the verse begins.

A necessary consequence of the occult character of the scripture is that the teachings therein, taken in their merely literal sense, are often likely to be misunderstood and sometimes grossly misused. I cannot better illustrate this observation than with reference to the first out of the four maxims, which form the introduction to a similar occult priceless little book called "Light on the Path" published more than thirty years ago in London. The maxims run: " (1) Before the eyes can see they must be incapable of tears. (2) Before the ear can hear, it must have lost its sensitivity. (3) Before the voice can speak in the presence of the Masters, it must have lost its power to wound. (4) Before the soul can stand in the presence of the Masters, its feet must be washed in the blood of the heart." These statements are descriptions of an aspirant who is seeking to enter the path leading to *Moksha or Nirvana* or liberation and thus wishes to become a disciple of one of those Great Teachers, who are ever ready to take in hand and train up all who are fit for being initiated into the mysteries of nature, of God and the soul. For, such teachers themselves proclaim: " Those who have passed through the silence, (which marks the blood of the soul) and felt its peace and retained its strength they long that you shall pass through it also"[2]. The qualifications above mentioned, expressed in the fewest words, are true sight, true hearing, true speech and true capacity to render service- not service to the teachers themselves, for they stand in no need of such personal attention, but to the world at large, of which they are the spiritual guardians.

Taking now the said first maxim, nothing can be simpler than it, so far as the mere words go; but if understood literally, the aphorism will lead to disastrous conclusions. For, it would amount to recommending absolute hard- heartedness, lack of sympathy and compassion. But, such an attitude on the part of the aspirant cannot but, on the very face of it, be an obstacle to his ardently wished for spiritual growth and not a help. To be incapable of tears with reference to the suffering of another is the method by which the dark path is to be trodden. It is the path of which one by-product, familiar to us all, is the Prussian super-man, who is now vigorously endeavouring to uproot all civilization. The development of the man , treading this dark path is by contraction, leading finally to that terrible state of isolation called *avichi;* than which no greater calamity can befall a human Ego. What then is the sense in which the man wishing to tread the White Path – the Path to Nirvana – is to be incapable of tears? The answer is he should be completely above being moved even in the slightest degree by untoward happenings to himself and which would cause anguish, sorrow and mental suffering, if he were an ordinary man of the world. This is not all. His soul has to become "as the ripe mango fruit as soft and sweet as its bright golden pulp for others' woes" on the one hand, and on the other as hard "as that fruit's stone for his own throws and sorrows." Of course, this habit of keeping under complete check, man's emotional nature in one particular direction while at the same time. That nature is sustained fully alive and keen, is not easily acquired. But he, who aspires to tread the path to the most exalted Goal before him, cannot but assiduously strive for the formation of such a faculty. Because, it is to be remembered his growth is to be by expansion of his knowledge and the power to serve. It is when all these reach their highest pitch of perfection that he can merge himself in the Divinity whose Will is at work in the particular part of the cosmos and become a co-worker with it.

To make the present discussion complete, it remains to add that there is a very marked distinction between the sympathy with the afflictions of his fellow- men felt by a disciple and that proceeding from one who has reached liberation. In the former case, the sympathy is ever attended with regret, while in the latter, it is otherwise. The fully illuminated soul sees and knows, as none below its level on the evolutionary ladder can see and know, that what we call afflictions are but necessary incidents in a man's growth, and thus within the Divine scheme of his evolution. Consequently, the regret which was occasioned in the disciple by the absence of full comprehension of that scheme, finds no place in the mind of him, whose vision is utterly unclouded and perfect. In his case, it is compassion, unalloyed, spurring him on, to an enlightened co-operation with God's plan by endeavours to remove that nescience, which is at the root of all the errors of the yet-developing humanity. It is not until this final stage – that of Nirvana – is reached that the regret which accompanies a disciple's sympathy can altogether cease, though such regret will continue to diminish at each of the four great stages of the progress of the human Ego. Those stages, needless to add, are *Parivrajaka, Kuteechaka, Hamsa and Parama- Hamsa,* in terms of Hindu nomenclature with the corresponding Buddhistic names *Shrottapatti, Sakridagamin, Anagamin and Arhat.* When the four true great initiations, marking the above tages have been undergone, and the Ego attains to the superhuman fifth stage, that of the *Tureeyateeta* , he becomes an *Asekha* (I,e,. one who has nothing more to learn in the world system to which he belongs.). It may not be out of place to point out that at the said initiations, the fortunate Ego concerned is given certain " Keys to Knowledge " and "words of power" which, among other things, enable him to progress along the path to liberation he is treading – a path as narrow and sharp as a razor, as the Upanishad expresses it. In all this, there is no question of favour. The wonderful expansion of consciousness and soul purification, which the Ego has been able to effect by strenuous efforts birth after birth, entitle him to those keys and words as a matter of simple justice. This is never withheld from him even for a minute after it is due. Neither arbitrariness nor partiality of any sort nor delay is possible in things of such moment to humanity, governed, as they are, by laws administered by the all wise and merciful Hierarchy, consisting of Manu, Vyasa and other less known Adhikara Purushas, under the guidance of that Mighty Being who is the spiritual King and Lord of our globe. Many are His manes in the sacred books. For example, in the Mahabharata He is almost uniformly spoken of as Narayana. In the Chandogya Upanishad text beginning with the words *ahara Suddhow*, His titles are *Sanat kumara and Skanda*. And the words therein *Tamasahparam Darsayati* (shows the light beyond the darkness) amply justify the very apt names applied to Him in some modern English writings, namely the One Initiator.

It will be seen from what I have been explaining above that the aphorism I have commented on, though extremely simple at first sight, requires much diving into, if misconception is to be avoided. And it follows that many of the teachings of the Geeta, owing to their occult nature, stand in need of like effort on the part of the student, if their true import is to be understood. Now, in passing, it is hardly necessary to remark that, in the hands of those, in whom there is no real yearning for spiritual growth and whose minds are not mature enough to grasp the deep significance of the teachings, the Geeta could serve no useful purpose whatever. In some few cases of this description, unmixed evil may result from some of the precepts being understood literally, as for instance, in the case of the misguided youths who have been made to believe that the injunction " O, Arjuna, fight" which occurs so often in the course of the political crimes they are guilty of as part of the plot to overthrow the British Raj. How can these unwary youths be expected to realize that the battle to be fought is not as against intimate friends and near relatives as the words on their face suggest but those emotions of men, personified as such in the narrative at the commencement of the book- emtioons which are hindrance to spiritual progress, namely *raga, dvesha, lobha, moha, mada , matsarya* and so on which have been nurtured for ages through countless births and re-births. The case of these unfortunate youths forms another illustration of the wisdom of the saying " Throw not pearls before swine." What I have thus tried to indicate and much more, would be found to indicate and much more, would be found emphatically stated in the verse which be found emphatically stated in the verse which lays down to what classes of person the Geeta should not be taught. Turning now to the case of those who are more or less fit to enter upon the study of the scripture, it should be borne in mind that some of the most important precepts admit of more than one interpretation, each being legitimate from its own point of view. In support of this position, let me take for example, that crucial word which is so conspicuous in it throughout, namely, Yoga. No doubt in one view, and indeed a very essential one, it is that *Samatvam* which is the man a complete mastery not only over his thoughts, emotions and activities, but also invests him with an unlimited capacity for and power of utterly selfless service. This is certainly a consummation to be devoutly wished. But is that all the term under discussion connotes and was meant to connote? Is there not a far more glorious *Samatvam,* necessarily implied by the word *Samadhi,* which is the very end and aim of all Yoga according to the very highest authorities? The answer to this question must emphatically be in the affirmative. To hold otherwise would be tantamount to saying that the Geeta, a veritable Upanishad itself, is in this respect in direct conflict with the whole trend of Hindu sacred literature. Now, the equipoised condition, just above mentioned, has reference to what is known as the *jagrat avastha, i. e.,* in words intelligible to us all, the state of our waking or the ordinary brain consciousness. The existence, however, of other states of consciousness cannot be denied even by the most skeptical; as for instance, the dream condition and that of deep undisturbed sleep *svapna and sushupti* known to everyone. Into the question of what the real facts of these states are, it is unnecessary to enter here. What however is relevant in the present connection is that *Tureeya[3]* or the fourth state which is universally asserted by Hindu writers to be the *summum bonum.* Nowhere is this state more accurately and tersely described than in thse well – known passages of the Mandukya Upanishad which begin with the words *Nantah-prajnam* and end with *sa vijneyah.* In this matchless description of the subject, the Sruti first negates that the *avastha* in question is any of the conditions of consciousness within the experience of ordinary men. Next, it points out that state is incapable of being perceived by any of our senses. And it winds up with the following affirmative explanations: *Ekatma- pratyayasaram* – the essence, the fount of all the individual Selves; *Prapanchopasamam* – wherein the three lower states -

Jagrat, Svapna and Sushupti - merge and cease; *santam* - peace; *sivam* - where the creative preservative and disintegrating or reabsorbing forces worketh not; *bliss* - *advaitam* - non-duality. By way of refusing the possible objections, such a state is not- existent or unknowable, the Sruti affirms, " It is the Self, It is knowable and ought to be known - *sa atma sa vijneyaha.* " The fact that the term Atma is the Geeta, as well as in every other Hindu sacred book, synonymous with the all – important part of Brahman, when viewed in its divided form of *Atma, Prakriti and Shakti,* must necessarily warrant the conclusion that the *Tureeya* state was recognized as completely by the Geeta as by the other scriptures of the highest authority. Nor is this *Tureeya* state a matter of Hindu teaching alone. It is the buddhistic Nirvana, misunderstood as utter extinction, but which is rest in Omniscience, as it has been felicitous phrased. It is the state wherein, as Christian writers would express it, the Peace that passes the understanding abides. The attainment of complete experience of this ineffable state is necessarily the work of ages for a human soul. But the beginnings thereof take place during the first of the great initiations. Thenceforward conscious functioning becomes possible in *Janalika* composed of the matter of the Vayu plane infinitely finer than that of this dense earth. Those beginnings are described in Light on the Path from which the following few eloquent sentences are worth citing: " Then will come a calm such as when nature works so swiftly that one may see her action. Such calm will come to the harnessed spirit. And in the deep silence, the mysterious event will occur which will prove that the way has been found. Call it by what name you will, it is a voice that speaks where there is none to speak – it is a messenger that comes, a messenger without form or substance; or it is the described by any metaphor. But it can be felt after, looked for, and desired , even amid the raging of the storm. The silence may last a moment of time or it may last a thousand years. But it will end. Yet you will carry its strength with you. Again and again, the battle must be fought and won" (pp. 21-23). Surely it is this final state that is reached in *Samadhi* which is the ultimate aim of Yoga according to all authorities. Hence, in this highest I Samadhi, comprehended by the term Yoga there lies the deepest layer of the " heart of the Geeta" to be probed and penetrated by him, who has the requisite spiritual faculty to fathoms it.

In justice to the view I have ventured to put forward above, it is necessary that I should refer to one more instance supporting it, that instance however being not transcendental as the one explained in the last paragraph. I would here invite the reader's attention to the well-known verse with which the dialogue concludes according to the recession, now almost universally in use. The two most important words in the verse are "*mam*" and "*aham*." Now one set of students will take both to refer to Shri Krishna, the Avatar. From their point of view, as aspirants who stand in need of a personal God to lean upon, the Avatara will necessarily appeal to them as what the terms stand for. But other students, who have risen above such a need and to whom, only that which is impersonal and philosophically worthy of acceptance would appeal, must seek a different explanation of the terms. And they will find it in the incontestably right interpretation offered, for example, in the remarkable commentary called Hamsa Yogi's *Bhashya* not much known as yet but which, I hope, circumstances permitting, to get published before long. According to this illuminating commentary, "*mam*" signifies that aspect of *Brahman* spoken of in the Geeta as *Daivi Prakriti* , identified with the Holy Ghsot of Christian Trinity, as for instance Swami T. Subba Row's learned discourses on the Geeta, delivered so far back as 1886. This Daivi Prakriti is the same as the *Nirupadhikam Mahachaitanyam* of some of the Hindu scriptures. Infinite becoming supreme potency *Bahu Bhavana Maha Sakti* is one of its many apt names. The aptest of them are those used during the daily twilight prayers of the Aryan, viz., *Savitri* - the World – mother; *Saraswati* - the Fountain head of Wisdom and Knowledge; *Gayatri* - the Redeemer and Saviour. In short it is the One or Cosmic Life, animating all manifested existence, as indicated by the Geeta words,

अपरेयमितस्त्वन्यां प्रकृतिं विद्धि मे पराम्।

जीवभूतां महाबाहो ययेदं धार्यते जगत्॥VII.5॥

" *Jiva bhutam mahabaho yayedam dhaayate jagat.* " The purport of this part of the teaching in question, in so far as the more developed student is concerned, is that utter freedom from the heresy of separateness coupled with complete devotion[4] to the Mahachaitanyam is the way to the one Supreme Self, the *atma* aspect of *Parabrahman* connoted by the other term "*aham*." That the same doctrine is the one accepted in all true occult schools of India at least, an earnest enquirer can satisfy himself. By way of one example, reference may be made to the Prayer to be mentally offered on rising in the early morning by an aspirant undergoing the discipline in vogue among the members of the Suddha Dharma Mandala. It runs " *abhedanandam, Chitram Param Brahma Veda Saha yo Avyayatma Samachitta Rangah, Daiveem Kalyana Shaktim Prapadya Sarvam Pravisati Amritoham,*

Ajaroham Lokebhyas Sukham Edhatam. " Next as to the term " *aham *," as already observed , it connotes for the advanced student the *Paramatman,* the One Self in all the cosmos and in particular residing in every human heart. This interretation is unquestionably warranted by what appears in many other verses of the scripture. Suffice to refer to the verse commencing with the words " *Aham Atma Gudakesa"* and in which the term under consideration is explained is explained to be the One Universal Self. It is this interpretation alone that could lead to the final truth that a man's salvation is to be sought from the Divinity within himself and not from any external source whatsoever. That final truth is nowhere more impressively expressed than in a passage in the beautiful little book, called "Idyll of the White Lotus"emanating from the same source, that gave Light on the Path to the English speaking public. In a speech purporting to be addressed by the spiritual Teacher who took part in the initiation of an advancing soul, the former said "Hear me, my brother, there are three truths which are absolute, and which cannot be lost, but yet may remain silent for lack of speech. The soul of man is immortal and its future is the future of a thing whose growth and splendor has no limit, "The Principle which gives life dwells in us, and without us, is undying and eternally beneficent, is not heard or seen or smelt but is perceived by the man who desires perception. Each man is his own absolute law-giver, the dispenser of glory or gloom to himself; the decreer of his life, his reward, his punishment. These truths, which are as great as is life itself, are as simple as the simplest mind of man. Feed the hungry with them. Farewell."

I trust it will be conceded on all hands that the statement with which I started the present part of the discussion to the effect that important terms in the Geeta comprehend and are intended to comprehend ideas widely differing from each other though connected by some circumstances common to them, is absolutely well founded.

It now remains to advert to two things calculated to be helpful in a fruitful study of the scripture. As to the first of them, the one comparatively less important, that has reference to the real source of the teachings imparted in the book. In this connection, certain material statement occurring in the Geeta or in other places in the Mahabharata, have to be taken into consideration and read between the lines, as intuitive students should always read such passages. For, statements of such description are often allegorical, or by way of parables and rarely direct matter of fact presentations of the truths intended to be conveyed. The statements to be considered are ---

1. Sanjaya's saying that through the grace of Vyasa, he was enabled to hear the actual delivery of the discourse by Shri Krishna.
2. That Shri Krishna and Arjuna were no other than Narayana and Nara , the mighty Rishis ever engaged in Tapas in Badari, intentupon the welfare of the world.
3. That the substance of the discourse was no more than primeval teachings to humanity.
4. That the discourse took place on the eve of what has to be spoken of as the Kali -age.

Putting these various statements together the student cannot but draw the following conclusions : --

1. That the discourse, stripped of its dramatic garb, was an inspired message from the Spiritual King of our Globe, *Narayana to Nara* or the humanity under his charge.
2. That this message was called forth by the cyclic change taking place at the time when it was vouchsafed.
3. That, that time was about the beginning of the colonization of India by the branch of the Aryan race which came to it from their original home in Central Asia in the neighbourhood of the sacred Shamballa, sanctified by the holy presence in it of Narayana, though in a form invisible to mortal eyes.

If the student will bear the above facts in mind, and meditate, as a preliminary to the commencement of his study for the day, upon the mighty source from which the scripture has emanated, he will necessarily put himself *en rapport* with that source and will receive such inspiration as the intensity of his aspirations and his purity entitle him to at the ever-merciful hands of the Spiritual Hierarchy, watching over our humanity. The programme for this preliminary step will be found well described in the verses , constituting the *Gita – Parayana – karma*[5] [i] printed at page 2 of the Suddha Dharma Mandala edition.

Lastly as to the second and remaining helpful point; it consists in a firm resolve to live up to the teachings, and a persistent endeavor to carry them out so far as possible. Every effort to do so will not only throw light upon them but also go to show their value and utility, as beating upon the whole life of an aspirant. Take, for instance, the advice to look upon praise and blame with equal indifference, *Tulyanindastuti,* an advice identical in sense with the aphorism quoted from Light on the Path, " Before the ear can hear it must have lost its sensitiveness." Any one who has meditated upon this advice and tried not to be disturbed or upset by idle gossip or malicious slanders about himself will know how free he feels from the torments he used to suffer, previously, from such things said of him. As time goes on, he will also find that the elation, which praise brought him, affects him no longer, he having arrived at the unalterable conviction that what really matters is not the opinion of others about him, but the intrinsic worth of his own thoughts, words and deeds. In short, the Geeta is a book not, in the words of Becon, to be merely tasted, or to be swallowed, or even to be chewed and digested but is the teaching of the Lord, whose golden precepts must be lived, verily lived.

To conclude, if this great scripture is approached by an aspirant to spiritual progress on the lines which I have humbly endeavoured to indicate, it cannot but be productive of the most beneficial result not only to the people of this country whose special inheritance it is, but also to those others who are likely to be brought into touch with it, by treatises like the one coming from the erudite pen of His Holiness. I close with saying that I esteem it an honour to have been allowed to contribute this Foreword and am most thankful for the kind consideration thus shown to me.

Madras , 16th October 1918. S. SUBRAMANIEM.

[1] Meaning: in a way that is stated publicly;

[2] Light on the Path, notes to rule 21, page 23

[3] This classification of consciousness, into four states, has its origin in a universal principle. Each of these states finds expression in a corresponding plane or condition of matter forming interpenetrating spheres in space. For example, Jagrat consciousness, has Sthula or dense matter for its field of expression; Svapna consciousness has Sukshma or subtle matter; and Tureeya consciousness has sub- divisions; of which , the types are what we know as solid, liquid, gas and ether. And consciousness peculiar to each plane has sub-modes of expression too (e.g., Jagrat – Jagrat; Jagrat- Svapna; Jagrat- Sushupti; Jagrat – Tureeya. On the same analogy, vak, speech or sound is divided into para- subtleness; pashyanti – less subtle; madhyama – still less subtle; and vaikhari – dense or gross. This quadruple division has its foundation in the triune aspect of Divinity, Sat, Chit , Ananda or the " Good, the True and the

Beautiful" of Plato. Here as in order instances the sacred syllable Pranava is the symbol with its three matras or measures and the ardhamatra or the dot over the written letter O. in spite of all such classifications, it is needless to say, states of consciousness and corresponding planes of matter are infinite in their gradations in the cosmos. The main divisions are but those with characteristics greatly and deeply well – marked and unmistakably distinguishable from each other. There is a seven – fold division , peculiar to our world system and not universal. The names of these special forms of consciousness are: jagrat, svapna, sushupti, tureeya, nirvanic, para-nirvanic and maha-paranirvanic with corresponding lokas or regions. The understanding of the facts of Nature, enumerated above, cannot but be useful to one who is intent upon self study. For, his bodies, visible and invisible, make up a microcosm governed by the same rule and laws as the great cosmos outside him.

[4] The statement "renouncing all dharma surrender unto mam alone" is one requiring much explanation. Though that cannot be attempted here, a few words are necessary to guard against serious misconception on the point. The devotion contemplated by the verse is, of course, not mere religious worship with or without rites. It is complete dedication of the whole life of the aspirant towards carrying out as far as it lies in him, the Divine Will, which is expression itself in the evolutionary processes at work before his own eyes. The dedication necessarily involves the aspirants ceasing to be a mere pawn on a chess board as it were moved about hither and thither by his selfish or self centred motives. He must become a conscious co-worker with that Divine Will by strenuous performance of every duty small or great developing on him for the moment with reference to his fellow- men and the world at large. Such discharge of duty must be for the sake of the duty itself regardless of any supposed meritoriousness in the matter. This systemic and pointed regulation of his life directed solely towards the furtherance of God's plan and acting without desire for the fruit will necessarily make the aspirant a willing participator in the Divine work. This is fully developed in the verses in the scripture on Karma Yoga where it is pointed out that the aspirant who so strives reaches the supreme. The true significance of the important term Karma Yoga will be missed unless it is taken as the utilisation of all the aspirants' faculties of Ichcha, Gnana and Kriya so as to be productive of a harmonious result. It is the co-ordination of his feeling, thought and action towards helping to turn the Samsara Chakra or the evolutionary wheel, at which Ishwara is ever engaged, though He has nothing to gain by it that would constitute the practice of Karma Yoga of the highest order.

Such Yoga on the aspirant's part, incarnation after incarnation, makes the individual life of the Yogi an integral part of the Cosmic oor the One Life mam and which is no other than the manifest or energizing aspect of the Supreme Self, the Aham, in the verse. Hence the emphatic declaration in another part of the Geeta " after many many births the man of wisdom enters mam – bahunam janmanamante jnanavan mam prapadyante. " such an one becomes the possessor of wisdom by reason of his having realized that "all is the Self " – Vasudevas – sarvamiti. " In this context, "Vasudeva" is but a synonymn for Atma, thee Self, as is made to appear by the Lord's statement " jnana atmaiva mematam – my doctrine and teaching is the wise man is verily the Self. The union of the individual life with the One Life puts an end to the false notion of duality or the heresy of separateness the source of all delusions. The total cessation of that heresy results in the long longed for moksha or liberation in fulfillment of the final promise in the Geeta " the aham or the Self will releases you from all delusions, grieves not – aham twam sarva papebhyo moksha yishyami masuchah."

[5] According to the Parayanakrama referred to in the text, the student may notice that salutations have to be offered not only to Narayana and Nara and Krishna and Arjuna, but also to certain Hamsas. He may like to know who these Hamsas are. The point is worth briefly explaining, as it is one which throws light upon the general question of the origin of such scriptures as Brahmanas, Upanishads, Itihasas, Puranas etc.

The derivation of Hamsa, as pointed out in Yoga Deepika No . 2 of Suddha Dharma Mandala series is: " Ha" is Ahankara or the I- concept; "Ma" is the supreme Brahman; "Sa" stands for the science and art which teach that all see in all things the Eternal Self of the very nature of Parabrahman and the root of everything. In Dharma Deepika No. 4 of the said series, there are observations suggesting that, like the swan in the fable which has the faculty of separating the milk from the water, Hamsas bring out the true teachings hidden in the allegories, myths and the like, of which Hindu scriptures are so full. There is a statement in the Mahabharata to the effect that the Birthless One, in the form of a swan, taught Sadhyas the science and art of Brahman and established the office of Hamsa, charging those filling the office with the duty of imparting sacred instruction to the world. It will thus appear that Hamsas are members of the spiritual Hierarchy, whose functions are to sully the needs of humanity in relation to the sacred science and all knowledge in general, according to the exigencies of each age, race and the then conditions. The exact processes, by which they supply those needs, are matters upon which little is to be seems certain that Brahmanas, Upanishads, Itihasas, Puranas etc., as we possess them, owe their origin to the inspiration of these Hamsas and that accounts for the name "Sruti" – Heard, - applied par excellence to the two former classes of Hindu scriptures. Presumably, the actual recording of what is inspired by those custodians of knowledge, is done by men who are found by the Hierarchy to be fit instruments and channels for the transmission of the installments of knowledge, considered as needed for the time being. The persons chosen for the task, as might easily be judged, are necessarily more or less advanced souls, willing to be the channels of the Hierarchy under assumed names and to work unknown in the midst of those with whom their work lies. In some instances, such records have the name Hamsa itself applied to them, as for example, the commentary on the Geeta and numerous other works under the generic name of "Khandarahasya".

In these circumstances, it is not surprising that the labours of orientalists and scholars have been productive of small results, if any, with reference to the question of the actual authorship of Hindu scriptures and their chronology, etc.

In concluding this note, attention may be invited to those very instructive passages (quoted at pp. 31-32 of my Foreword to Yoga Deepika) from Dharma Deepika regarding the genesis of the Vedic chants, spoken of as Mantras of which Brahmanas and Uapnishads are explanations proceeding from the Hamsas as already stated.

Hence, in point of authority, Mantras stand first, Srutis next, Itihasas and Puranas last; an orderly succession perfectly intelligible to all who care to try and understand such things --

[i] These Mantras themselves are held to be revelations because they are the results of the deciphering by Rishis spoken of as Mantra Drashtaraha or Seers of Mantras. What are thus deciphered are so from the bulk of the immemorial records of all ages and climes enshrined as Dharma Deepika expresses it, in Akasic plates (Akasa palakay). It is portions of what are thus described which are handed down by Hierarchs of the highest rank, who go by the name of Vyasa – Arrangers – to races of mankind whose special needs they are calculated to serve and are accepted under the title of Veda.

Preface

Periods of catastrophe appear to be almost necessary at the present lives of mankind to awaken men from a stagnant conservatism in which they continue mechanically to follow their predecessors without conscious recognition of what they aim at or should aim at finally. The situation in the West, arrived at finally. The situation in the West, arrived at through ideals of national competition, dynasties and militarism, has aroused men throughout the world to a more serious and independent consideration of the meaning of life than at any time since the Renainsance of Learning. So again, in spite of a lip service to the excellence and superiority of its ancient wisdom, the East has imbibed too much of the scientific and critical methods of the West and caught too much its spirit of optimistic activity to feel that the traditional expression of its philosophies of life will still suffice . The actual situation in the West is sufficient proof that there are serious defects in its mode of life, and thus of the theories and ideals upon which it is based. The East cannot simply follow its own past, and it cannot be condemned for wishing to avoid the calamities which Western ideals have brought. All books of a practical religion and moral character must, therefore , in our day, be tested by the help that they give in relation to these pressing problems. The Bhagavadgita is concerned with questions so intimate and so persistent in the life of man that any honestly written book inspired by this Divine Lay may expect to find real appreciation in wide circles, especially of the Indian people. The Heart of the Bhagavadgita has a definitely practical aim in view: it discusses carefully the question as to the value of the Gita as a guide in practical life. The author is well –known to the Indian public as a most enlightened head of one of the monastic institutions associated with the name of the great monistic philosopher, Sankaracharya. To Western readers he may be introduced as the first man in such a position to give the world his reflection on this and many other subjects in a language in which they might be read in East and West. A genuine scholar, he is also the advocate of a modern expression of the truth of Hinduism. He is an incessant worker for a multiplicity of worthy causes having the welfare of India in view. The soundness of his judgment is seen by his deliberate abstention from discussions of doubtful value in the present work and the concentration of the reader's attention upon the practical teachings of the Gita. Western thinkers should read with interest the rule-or rather rules- of life which in a survey of an old and beloved Song, a modern Hindu proposes to a world in uncertainty as to that which belongs to its peace.

The ideal taught in this book has been recognised by all the great religions in one way or another. The expression given to it in English is "equanimity." "evenness of mind." Many attempts have been made by Western critics to interpret this in that sense of indifference for which nothing is worn while, or all is equally useless. It is not my intention to enquire whether or not there are good grounds for this position. What is more important is to note that the author in his teaching as in his active pursuit of worthy aims, is against such an interpretation. The hope may be expressed that Dr. Macnicol belongs to a type which is passing away, when he misrepresents the Hindu Ideal of a Holy Life as very largely one of a degrading indifference. The peace of mind referred to is real; it is by nature similar to what is meant by the Christian when he talks of "that peace which the world cannot give." It is quite another question whether Hindu thought is explicitly aware of what in Christian thought is called "Grace." Nevertheless, in the recognition of Bhakti or devotion is an opening for the acknowledgement of that personal relationship to Jesus which is central for Christians. The correct name of the religion of Muslims is Islam, the meaning of which again suggests peace and calm. Though the manner in which peace is supposed to come is different, through confidence and trust in submission to Allah, the thing aimed at and realised is essentially the same. And what is the Nirvana of the Buddhist but the state of equanimity of mind which comes with the transcendence of the anxiety of unsatisfied desire? These and other religions contain much more than such peace and calm; but in the times in which we live equanimity is an aspect of the ideal needing to be emphasized perhaps more than any other.

That this evenness of mind is not to be interpreted as a spirit of indifference, may easily be seen from the methods by which it is to be attained. In this connection it is worthy of note that The Heart of the Bhagavadgita breathes the same broad spirit as the work around which it is written. During the course of history, and none-the-less in recent years, frequent attempts have been made to present the teaching of the Gita in a one-sided fashion, usually teaching of the Gita in a one sided fashion, usually in supports of the special predilection of the writer. Whatever may eventually be the general verdict of scholars, here it is clear that for his definite purpose the author maintains a comprehensive and a psychological attitude: in varying degrees every man needs to make use of all the means, though for some men one path and for others other paths will lead most surely to redemption and peace. The insistence on this general type of interpretation, to the abandonment of a particularistic one, is in accordance with the tendency of modern though in East and West.

The rendering of each of the different forms of Yoga manifests a similar width of conception. Thus, the action which is implied in Karma Yoga is not taken , as some Western critics would like to represent it as always taken, as just external acts, the rites and rituals of religion, and the duties of caste. Rather, action is to be as "unattached" to caste as to anything else. Salvation is to be found by the performance of any or all possible good actions, whenever and wherever they are possible. If the people of the West need to learn to appreciate more the meaning of "equanimity," to subdue their feverish haste with a little more evenness of mind, the people of India need to learn more deeply to understand and to apply in actual life the doctrine of non-attachment, and of Karma-Yoga in the widest sense. Only thus will the depressing fact be overcome that so many Indians will do just what the actual requirements of their vocation demand, - and nothing else, unless the State or whoever else may be concerned, "makes it worth while." As I understand it the miserable discontent which exists so frequently in India is due very largely to the failure to recognise the equanimity, the salvation, which comes with a genuine understanding of Karma-Yoga and the doctrine of non-attachment.

Some few remarks are also needed with relations to the path of knowledge. Anyone who has seriously followed this path, even for a short period, will have experienced that freedom from care and that broadening of the outlook which come in concentrated study. There is no subject of intellectual enquiry which , with a modern interpretation, should not lead to Jnana- Yoga . The first reward of the search for knowledge is the search itself. Knowledge ought not to be convinced merely as concerned with the ultimate, the philosophy of the Absolute, or something thus metaphysical. The modern mind- as indeed, the human mind in all ages- recognises that the world of Maya, or whatever one may call it, deserves and demands consideration, and further, that in the pursuit of the knowledge of it some of the greatest human personalities have been developed and some of the most peaceful and happy moments of even ordinary individuals are found. Again the situation in this regard in India leaves much to be desired. Engaged as we are in this direction ourselves, the almost general neglect of research amongst the very numerous body of College professors and graduates is continually impressed upon us. A widespread repetition of a statement that the ancient Rishis were omniscient, and that all necessary knowledge can be found in the ancient books, serves as a cover for those who will not take the trouble to enquire into the accuracy of the claim. Offer a high salary and many will present themselves as qualified and as yearning to carry on research – in almost any subject one may like to suggest. Here, there is a great need for an appreciation of the salvation which comes through "knowledge for its own sake," for genuine understanding of Jnana – Yoga and the doctrine of non-attachment.

The main aim of The Heart of the Bhagavadgita may be considered almost entirely apart from any particular philosophical principles. The test of a practical aim must be the extent of the possibility of its achievement in practice. Yet to keep all questions of an ultimate metaphysical nature in the background is, after all, impossible even in the most practical of religious treatises. It would seem that it is in relation to the path of devotion that it is in relation to the path of devotion that the importance of these principles is mostly felt, for there comes into discussion the question as to what is an adequate Object for human adoration and love. And immediately the answer is given that God alone is an adequate Object, the inevitable problem of His nature arises. This problem cannot be pursued further here, but it becomes more and more clear that the appeal of the various religions to men will differ chiefly according to the form in which God is represented in them. In relation to these different forms the manner of expression of the devotees' love will vary. In East and West the need to follow the path of devotion more assiduously can hardly be denied. The "Christian" West may eventually find that its division and animosities and competition can only be overcome by making devotion to Jesus the mainspring of a life given to unseifish action and to knowledge. And the division and individualism of the East may only be transcended if a genuine understanding of Bhakti- Yoga in the spirit of noon-attachment be related to one recognised supreme Object of devotion in a common worship.

To me it seems that one passes into the mystical in the highest point of realisation of the life of action, of knowledge, and especially, of devotion. Mysticism is, I believe, as such beyond the scope of thought and language, so that I can say nothing concerning Dhyana – Yoga. The mystics always refer to their experiences as the highest bliss, and for the author it is certainly a condition of equanimity, of evenness of mind. That their experiences are real few careful students of human life will deny: the author insists in this book that these experiences only come to those who dispose themselves in a suitable mode of life. The reader will learn of this disposition from the author himself.

Baroda ALBAN G. WIDGERY

September 1918

Prologue

In the whole range of the world's literature, few books can be found which can favourably compare with "the Bhagavadgita" in point of interest or of influence.[1] This poem of seven hundred slokas embodies within its short compass as will be seen from the sequel, the best philosophy and the best religious and moral principles that Ancient India could offer to the world. The charmingly simple diction and the melody of the verses in which its loftiest teachings are clothed, make it a very fascinating study. The wonderful sequence with which the teachings are presented, the thought – stimulating phrases and clauses with which the work abounds, the popular mould in which the whole is cast, and the clearness with which the most sublime truths are propounded, make this one of the most interesting books.

It is a significant fact that from a very remote past down to our times, this sacred book of India has continued to exercise a very wide influence on not only the ordinary but also some of the most thoughtful minds. It is no wonder that it should have a great hold on the mind of the orthodox Hindu, for there is almost no traditional Indian ideal which is not here reverently handled and allotted an exalted place-worthy of it. Such of the Hindu commentators as had any literary and spiritual genius, found it hard to withstand the temptation of writing a commentary on the work. But that it should meet with the admiration and praise of the modern educated Hindus, and should have compelled the attention of the thoughtful Europeans and Americans, is a feature unparalleled in the whole history of Ancient Indian literature. Countless editions of the text see the light every year and are cordially welcomed by our countrymen. There is almost no Indian vernacular[2] which has not translated it, and no article or book on religion or philosophy which does not directly or indirectly draw its contents. Nay more, even social and political essays and articles written by patriotic Hindus of the present times may be said to often betray a strong passion for quotations from the Gita.[3] Then its influence upon the Westerns is by no means little.[4] The work has been translated into English,[5] Greek, Latin, Italian, French and German.[6][7]The practical nature of its teachings no less than the music of its language gives it a charm to the mind of the Europeans and Americans. The unusual respect paid to it by scholars reputed for their vast learning, indefatigable literary research and philosophic acumen, excited the attention of Christian Missionaries also. Some of them struck with the similarity of many of its teachings with those of the New Testament, have tried to prove that the Gita has borrowed its best ideas from the Bible.[8] Thus the book has received different treatment at different hands. The orthodox Hindu considers it a revelation and tries to follow its teachings, the modern educated Hindu commends it, and the European scholar admires it, while the Missionary tries to explain it away in any manner that suits his purpose. That this little book, the very time and authorship of whose composition is yet a matter of great difference of opinion among Scholars, [9] should be thus filled with unusual interest for men of different times and countries and of varying mental caliber, and that its influence on some of the most enlightened modern minds should be of such great magnitude, is a sufficient ground for any reflecting person to pause and ask himself, " *What is the valu of the Gita as a guide to practical life?*"

In the following pages an attempt will be made to answer this important question. Other phases of the study of the book will be subordinated to this main point, and will be dealt with only is so far as they affect it. No special research is claimed for the ideas here presented and no special school of philosophy is sought to be supported. No paragraph here will be devoted to establish or to refute the genuineness and historicity of the author, the hero and the incidents related in the book. No discussion will find a place herein which considers the vocabulary, the age and literary value, the inspired nature, the number of followers, the character, and social position of fame of the speaker or author of the Gita. It is not meant here that such considerations are utterly useless. They may have their own value to the philologist, to the historian or to the theologian. But to find an answer to the question proposed above, such enquiry is obviously quite unnecessary. We are only concerned here with the simple question whether the Gita has any practical wisdom to teach, whether its philosophy or theology can offer any practical method of self-culture. The book has therefore to be studied not from the too credulous orthodox, nor from the all – admiring patriotic standpoint, much less from the fault – finding view of critics. We have to approach the book much in the same manner as we would a treatise on Chemistry. Just as we would verify the thrust of the one by means of experiments, we should verify those of the other by an appeal to reason and experience. If reason vouchsafes the truth and if conscience approves of the ethics, we shall accept them and not otherwise.

The Title "Bhagavadgita"

The grammatical accuracy if the title "भगवद् गीता " deserves some careful investigation. The word GITA (गीता) is derived from GAI (गै) to song, of which it is the past passive participle. The termination TA(ता) might be also used in an abstract sense, in which case its gender would be neuter by Panini's rule "नपुंसके भावे कृत: ". With the termination "क्तनि् " another form GEETIH (गीति:) is also possible in the same sense. In the present case the word has taken the feminine termination टाप (आ) where it becomes evident that कृत is a passive participle termination and the whole word is therefore only an adjective requiring some feminine substantive to qualify. Hence the word MADBHAGVADGITA (मद्भगवद्गीता) by itself cannot form the full title of the work and is grammatically speaking incorrect.

This becomes more clear from an examination of the colophon at the end of each chapter which invariably runs "ॐ तत्सदिति श्रीमद्भगवद्गीतासूपनिषित्सु ब्रह्मविद्यायां योगशास्त्रे श्रीकृष्णार्जुनसंवादे." Now when the sentence is construed it will be found that the only word which is grammatically co-ordinate with मद्भगवद्गीतास् is उपनिषित्सु, the gender, number and case both being the same, while all other are independent in construction. Hence it is obvious that the expression BHAGAVADGITA (भगवद् गीता) is only a shortened form of BHGAVADGITOPANISHAD (भगवदगीतोपनिषिद) which is the full and correct title of the work, the plural perhaps being intended to refer to the Upanishadic doctrines propounded. [10] Gita is a further contraction used more often and we speak of "The Bhagavadgita" of " the Gita" meaning of course "the Bhagavadgitopanishad." This process of contraction is by no means rare in Sanskrit. Thus Vedavyasah is shortened into Vyasah (व्यास:) and Bheemsenah into bheemah (भीम:).

<u>*What is The Bhagavadgita?*</u>

The main question with which this essay has started gives room to another incidental point to be settled. What is the Bhagavadgita? This has to be decided at the vast outset, because on the answer to this question depends the pertinence of the main enquiry. It is a truism that no one would look for grammatical truths, in a treatise on medicine, or consult a book on Astronomy with the expectation of finding in it information on legal matters. Hence to be assured that we are justified in looking for practical ethics in the Gita, it is very essential to ascertain what the book is meant for. This question has been answered in different ways by different scholars.[11] Some think it a reconciliation of the warring religious sects of the times of the author. [12] Others see in it an endeavour to exalt the caste duties above all other obligations. [13]And some others hold that the Gita is meant to revive Krishnaism and emphasize the Krishnavatar. But it is curious that none of such views takes cognizance of what the author himself calls his work. In the colophon at the end of each chapter, he says: " Thus ends the chapter called so and so of the Upanishads sung by the Lord, which are the philosophy of Brahman and the Science of Yoga, as expounded in the course of the dialogue between Sri Krishna and Arjuna." The author clearly intends therefore that the book must be judged as a philosophy of Brahman and a Science of Yoga.

The question now assumes another shape. What is Brahman, and what is Yoga according to the Gita? "What is the Grahman you spoke of?" is the first of the seven questions which Arjuna is made to ask Sri Krishna at the beginning of the eighth chapter. The answer given is "Brahman is the Highest Unchangeable." In the thirteenth chapter again, a description of this Brahman is given, "I shall now tell you what ought to be known and knowing which one attain immortality. It is the beginning-less Highest Brahman." Then follows a long description carried on by means of seemingly contradictory assertions. From these two passages, we learn that the Brahman of the Gita is the Highest Reality that knows no change. Now for the term Yoga: As in the case of the word Brahman, the author refers to this word in two places, in one of which he defines the term, while in the other he gives a general description intended to convey to the readers' mind what is meant by the word. In the 48th verse of the second chapter, we read "समत्वम् योग उच्चते" "evenness is called Yoga." And in verses 20 to 23, chapter VI, we have the following description of Yoga. "Where the mind becomes quiescent, controlled by practice, where seeing the Self by Self one is satisfied in himself; where one experiences absolute bliss known only to the mind but ever beyond the senses; and standing where one swerves not from the truth; where no other gain is considered greater, and where placed one is not moved by the greatest pain that (state), a state in which there is the absence of all contact with misery, is to be understood by the term

Yoga."

In the whole of the Gita there is no other place where the terms Brahman and Yoga are made the subject of discussion, and there is no other definition or description of either term, though both the words are freely interspersed throughout the work. That in the shorter of the passages cited above, the terms are intended to be defined and that longer extracts are meant to be explanatory to the definitions, is corroborated by the following considerations:

The epithet "Paramam (परमम)" "Highest" of Brahman in the definition is recognized in the descriptive passage by the word "Param (परम)" which also means Highest, and in both the contexts Brahman is considered as the great Reality to be known. This is not the case, for instance, in the passage "मम योनरि्महत्वम" where, though the epithet "Mahat (महत)" "great" is used, Brahman evidently denotes something other than the Reality; so also with Yoga. The definition identifies it with "Evenness" and though the term "YOGA" primarily meaning "connection" is here used by what is called वपिरीत लक्षण (indication by the opposite) to denote separation of दुःखसयंोग (the contact of misery.)[14] In fact a little further on in the same chapter comes this passage which makes the assurance doubly sure. "योऽयं योगस्त्वया प्रोक्तः साम्यने मधसुूदन। एतस्याहं न पश्यामि चअ्चलत्वात् स्थति िस्थरिम्॥6.33॥" " This Yoga described by you as *evenness,* Oh, Slayer of Madhu, I cannot see how it can remain permanent, seeing that the mind is fickle."

Our investigation therefore leads us to the following conclusion. Brahman is the Highest Reality or Truth and Yoga is evenness of mind in which the Truth is seen. Brahma- Vidya is thus the Philosophy of the Real and Yoga – Sastra is the science of equanimity, perfect equanimity being according to the Gita the one condition in which the mind can have access to the Real. What does the "Bhagavadgita" profess to be then? It proposes to put forth the theory of the Real, and to recommend a line of conduct which will lead us to the realization, the Gita calls Yoga. Whatever leads up to this Yoga is also called Yoga by transference of the term. Thus each chapter of this book deals with a separate Yoga, though the ultimate aim is the Yoga properly so called, to wit, equanimity.[15] Yoga has several other meanings in Sanskrit, but when we talk of the Yoga of the Gita, we had better dissociate all such meanings from this word.

Yoga S'astra

The bulk of the Gita is taken up with the Yoga Sastra rather than with Brahma Vidya, though as we have said the work itself claims to be both. Philosophical truths are adduced here more for the purpose of supporting the Yoga doctrines rather than for entering upon an intellectual discussion of philosophical problems. It is not that the intellect is given a low place in the Gita, nor that the glorious results of rational enquiry are here held up for ridicule or contempt, but the results of all philosophic enquiries are made the very basis of its chief subject, the Yoga. Philosophy is brought down to the lower level of every day experience without losing even a ray of its lustre, and its truths are here presented in such a simple manner and as it were in such a concrete form that the commonest minds can understand them and put them into daily practice. It is very often said with reference to Indian philosophy that it aims at something beyond this world and ignores the present life, that it asks us to give up life if we wish t cure the evils of life, and that it is, in short, merely an impracticable theory promising a state of perpetual happiness after death in reward for an utter neglect of the practical life. The Gita is the one standing protest to this baseless charge. Its object is to show how the highest of the Vedantic truths are at the same time the simplest of all, how every one of them can be applied and meant to be so applied to this very practical work-a-day world and how religious means no more than philosophy applied to everyday life. The Gita as a Yoga Sastra or Science of Yoga, shows how, in whatever stations of life we may be, and whatever may be our intellectual capacity , each one of us may understand and live religion to the extent of our capability, every minute of our life. Nay more, the Yoga Sastra of the Gita is mainly intended to show that here in this very life is to be sought the highest beatitude and further to point out that there is really not so much antagonism between religion and the life of the world as is commonly fancied. This statement may be received at first with some doubt by a portion of our readers, but the sequel, it is hoped, will place it on surer foundations. For the present we may state the Yoga Sastra tries to explain the practical part of Vedanta and to offer an ideal character to be realized.

The practicality of the Gita consists in its recognising the varieties of minds and inclinations. Though truth is one, and the ultimate goal must be the same, yet it cannot be insisted that all must follow the same method to reach it. Though perfect health is the goal of all his patients, a doctor would not prescribe the same course of treatment to them all. Several things would have to be taken into consideration, age, sex, present state of health, as well as the general habits of the patient. Similarly, a religion to be practicable to a large portion of mankind should be ready to supply the need of various minds that seek it. This is what the Gita attempts to do. It classifies religious aspirants into four divisions, the active man, the emotional man, the mystic and the man of reason. These four classes are not mutually exclusive of one another, for all the four characteristics do actually exist in every mind to some extent or other. The classification however is based on the predominance in individual souls of one of the four natures, and though no two minds may be said to be exactly similar in all particulars, yet the Gita considers that for all practical purposes, it will be sufficient to divide human minds into these four types. And there is a Yoga for each of these types; though the goal to be attained is in each case the same.

The Ideal of the Gita

And what is this goal? This question has received several answers from the various Acharyas who have commented on the Gita. It is said by some that is the great ideal of the Gita, Gita being sometimes called the Gospel of duties. Others say that love is regarded as the great ideal of life by the author of Gita. Some others declare that knowledge is the goal, while yet others maintain that meditation is its ultimate aim.

Now, there are passages in the Gita, which taken by themselves confirm each of these views. Let us take "work" for instance.

It is said in in II- 47 ,

कर्मण्येवाधिकारस्ते मा फलेषु कदाचन।

मा कर्मफलहेतुर्भूर्मा ते सङ्गोऽस्त्वकर्मणि।। II.47 ।।

"Yours is only to work." Again in chapter III, we have "Regularly perform your work, for action is better than inaction." "Working without attachment, man attains the highest." "Janaka and others attained perfection solely through work." This view has not only the sanction of the texts such as those quoted just now, but also stands to reason; for is it not quite natural that one should work for what one wants to reach? No one but a lazy person would expect to find the goal without work. Again, take "love.": This side too, has its texts. In chapter V, we read, "It is they that get absorption in Brahman, who have absconded their doubts, who are self-controlled and who ever love all beings." In XI, it is stated, "He who is free from hatred towards every being reaches Me." In XII again, "They reach Me only, for they are ever bent on doing good to all beings."

These and other similar passages point to universal love as the ideal and reason also supports it. For, there can be really no good work except through a motive of love, and the best thinkers of all times have preached and rest of mankind have given their assent to nothing but universal love as the means of eradicating the evil of life. Meditation or concentration of thoughts also claims the support of the Gita. "There is neither enlightenment nor religion fervour for one who has no concentration; and for one without any fervour no peace can come; whence happiness without peace?" Again, we are told in VI, "Applying himself thus constantly, the Yogin gains control over his mind and obtains the peace and blessedness of My Estate." The Yogin is said in the next Sloka to be greater that ascertain, greater than intellectual man, and greater than workers. This side too therefore, can make out a strong case in favour of it. Reason is ready to support it. For, what do all achievements represent but degrees of mental-concentration? All knowledge is acquired by concentration of mind, that is, by fixing the mind exclusively on the particular subject of enquiry. So, concentration may also be said to be the ideal. As for knowledge, we have numerous Gita texts in its favour too. "All actions Oh! Partha, finds its culmination in knowledge." "The Jnanin is My very Self." And so on we find numerous other texts eulogizing knowledge; and reason has everything to say on the side of knowledge, for, reason itself is based on previous knowledge and in its turn is the accumulator of fresh knowledge. Work, love and concentration may be easily shown to lead to knowledge, and therefore on this side also, a very good position is made out, for those holding that knowledge is the ideal. Now, as we have already seen, there are four chief types of mind in this world, and it is natural that each one should have a different aim according to his particular inclination. And if we consider the other varieties of minds also for which there is ample room in this world of ours, we should be hardly surprised to find that there are numerous and different goals for which they are severally making.

And the Gita supports all these! So, we have a medley of ideals all supported by Gita texts! "IS there no way out?" "Does not the Gita then recognise the superiority of any one ideal over the others?" this is the natural question that should now possess our mind, and the answer is very simple. Each one of these ideals is called a Yoga by the Gita and the Gita is the Science of Yogas. It is very object is to reconcile all the views. It is very object is to reconcile all the views. And how does it effect this reconciliation? Is it by raising any one of them into distinction and allowing that Yoga to lord over others? No. In the solution of this most vital of problem lies the practicality of the Gita, which is the greatest commentary yet written on Vedanta. Persons ignorant of the true tenor of the Gita have tried to make it a sectarian treatise, and by twists and tortures of slokas, they have attempted to produce proof- texts in their favour. The Gita has been made by such men to support by turns, work and no work, love and indifference, reason and mystic practice. But there is not one of these theories which does not take only a part and neglects the rest of the work. Taken as a whole, the Gita can never be made to support any one of the theories exclusively. It supports all ideals or none. No one sectarian can claim the special sanction of the Gita in his favour. Knowledge, work, love, concentration are all here commended but none at the expense of the others.[16]

People very often quarrel over words rather than facts. Even very intelligent men sometimes fight with one another, for the reason that some of them do not choose to set forth ideas in exactly the same words as others. An amusing story is related to four boys who were given a coin that they might purchase and equally divide among themselves some fruit they liked best. Each wanted to purchase the same fruit, but not knowing the language of one another, they began to quarrel, as each boy insisted on purchasing the fruit he named. Only the names were different: but they did not know it. At last, a man who knew all the four languages showed them the fruit itself and they were all equally glad and satisfied that each of them had at last carried his point. They then gave up quarreling when they found out their mistake and saw that all the four words stood for the same fruit and not for different things as they had supposed. Somewhat similar to this is the reconciliation effected by the Gita. Truth is the fruit of all the four ideals described above. Work leads to truth, concentration leads to truth, knowledge leads to truth and love leads to truth. All the four are real indeed. In fact each is an aspect of the same thing. To start with, they may appear different but they all finally converge to one point and then it is seen that each of them involves the others.

This point of convergency is called Yoga by the Gita. To attain that state of mind is to attain Yoga. This state has been defined by the author of the Gita in a single word "evenness." The mind has to reach a point where it is not affected by any external circumstances. As it is, the mind is subject to a thousand and one changes and the goal is to transform it into a state of "evenness." Every change is limiting the mind, and the ideal of the Gita is to train the mind so as to transcend as far as possible all such limitations. The process may be whatever is suited to the individual and each such process is called a Yoga, because it leads to the real Yoga, which is "evenness." No one can hope to reach this "evenness," until he has come to combine in him the ideal of work, concentration, knowledge and love. We have now to enter upon a more detailed study of each of these four Yogas of the Gita, in order to understand how the real ideal is reached through them.

[1] *Cf. " In the whole literature of the world there are few poems worthy of comparison, either in point of general interest, or of practical influence, with the Bhagavadgita. It is a philosophical work, yet fresh and readable as poetry, etc." (Ch. 1, Gita and Gospel by Rev J. N. Farquhar, M. A., Formerly Exhibitioner, Christ Church, Oxford).*

[2] *" Such is the estimation in which the work is held both in Asia and Europe, that it has been translated into Hindi, Telugu, Kannada and other European language and is also well known by European translators, of which Sir C. Wilkins, published in London in 1785, was the first." Footnote to p. 124. " Indian Wisdom." By Sir Monier Williams.*

[3] *" This revival of interest in Krishna and his worship is clearly part of the great national movement which has been so potent in Bengal religiously, socially and politically these last twenty years." Appendix to Gita and Gospel, by Rev. J. N. Farquhar, M. A.*

[4] *" The poem has also received a great deal of attention and admiring recognition from Europeans." Appendix to Gita and Gospel.*

[5] *" It was the first piece of Sanskrit literature ever translated into English. This translation was by Charles Wilkins, and appeared as early as 1785, under the title of The Song of the Adorable One. Since then it has been frequently brought before the English public," etc. Gita and Gospel, Ch I.*

[6] *Among the principal translation in European language other than English may be mentioned the Greek version of Galanos, the Latin version of Lassen, the Italian version of Stanisallo Gatti, the French version of Burnouf and the German version of Dr. Lorinser.*

[7] *"The lofty sublimity to which it so often rises the practical character of much of its teaching, the enthusiastic devotion to the one Lord which breathes through it and the numerous resemblances it shows to the words of Christ, fill it with unusual interest for men of the West." Gita and Gospel , Ch. I.*

[8] Sir Monier Williams hesitates " to concur in any theory (such as the one proposed by Dr. Lorinser, Prof. Weber and others) which explains these coincidence by supporting that the author had access to the New Testament or he derived some of his ideas from the first propagators of Christianity." He quotes the Rev. F. W. Farrar who in his interesting and valuable work " Seekers after God" points out " that the attempts of the Christian Fathers to make out Pythagoras a debtor to Hebraic wisdom, Plato an Atticizing Moses, Aristotle a picker up of ethics from a Jaw , Seneca a correspondent of St. Paul, were due "in some cases to ignorance, and in some to a want of perfect honesty in controversial dealing," and concludes that " his (Rev. Farrar's) arguments would be even more conclusive if applied to the Bhagavadgita." Vide p. 142, Indian Wisdom.

Also see " Dr. Lorinser's attempt (Die Bhagavadgita, ubersetz and erlautert von Dr. F. Lorinser, 1869) to prove that the author of the Gita borrowed many ideas from the Bible must be pronounced a failure. Cf. Garbe, 19, 83-85; Max Muller, Natural Religion, 87-100. Hopkins R. I., 429." Footnote to page 4, Gita and Gospel.

[9] I quite agree with my friend Dewan Bahadur J. S. Chakravarti, M.A., F.R.A.S., Comptroller, Mysore Government, who in his introduction to his lamented father Rai Bahadur Bireswar Chakravarti's translation (in Rhyme) to the Bhagavadgita, says: " There are, on the one hand, writers like Telanga, who after a careful and elaborate examination of the question of the question come to the conclusion that "the date at which the Gita can have been composed must be earlier than the third century B. C., though it is impossible to say how much earlier;" on the other hand, we have scholars oof the stamp of Lorinser, Weber nd Lassen who hold "that the Bhagavadgita was not written before the scholars who have written on the subject are men of vast scholarship, indefatigable industry and clear judgment no one can, for a moment, doubt; but all of them cannot be said to have been altogether free from bias."

[10] "It is, however, stayed an Upanishad or rather a series of Uanishads, because, like the Upanishads, it reveals secret and mystical doctrines." Foot — note 4 to page 125. "Indian Wisdom," by Sir Monier Williams.

Both the singular and plural forms of the word Bhagavadgita also seem to have been used by authoritative writers like Sankaracharya.

[11] . " They both (the Bhagavadgita and the Swetaswataropanishad) aim at reconciling the conflicting views of different systems, and both do so by attempting to engraft the Sankhya and Yoga upon Vedanta doctrine." " Indian Wisdom," p. 123.

So also Prof. Max Muller who sees in the Bhagavadgita a reconciliation of the philosophies of Yoga and Sankhya, though unlike Sir Monier Williams, Prof. A Macdonell and others, he holds that the word Sankhya – Yoga denotes only one philosophy.

[12] See " Summary of the Bhagavadgita" in " The Religious and Moral Teaching of the Bhagavadgita examined," by John Murdoch.

[13] " But the leading idea of the Gita is that Krishna is Brahma incarnate, round that all the rest of the teachings gathers" Gita and Gospel, p. 15.

[14] Possibly on the strength of this description (तं विद्याद् दुःखसंयोगवियोग योगसञ्ज्ञतिम्) and professedly on the latter half of an introductory verse by Bhoja in his commentary on the Yoga Sutras, Prof. Max Muller remarks that Yoga means not union but disunion. But Patanjali himself says in his aphorism that the term in his science only denotes the restraint of the modifications of the mind (योगश्चित्तवृत्तनिरोधः) And word "API(even)" in the above quotation from Bhoja which the Professor has simply passed over, clearly shows that Bhoja , by no means, took "separation" as a distinct signification of the term "Yoga." This view is made all the stronger by the word "APOORVA" (peculiar) in the first half of the same verse.

[15] It will become clear as we go on, how this definition of "Yoga" as equanimity, equally applies to Jnana – Yoga, Karma – Yoga and other Yogas.

[16] सांख्ययोगौ पृथग्बालाः प्रवदन्ति न पण्डिताः।
एकमप्यास्थितः सम्यगुभयोर्विन्दते फलम्॥5.4॥
यत्सांख्यैः प्राप्यते स्थानं तद्योगैरपि गम्यते।
एकं सांख्यं च योगं च यः पश्यति स पश्यति॥5.5॥

It is to be noted that the word Sankhya is the Gita stands for Jnana, but not for the system of philosophy (by Kapila) technically so called. This view is shared not only Oriental authorities like Sri Sankaracharya but also by some of the occasional critics like Dr. Paul Deussen who in his Outlines of Indian Philosophy says "The words (Sankhya and Yoga) are thus (i.e., in the sense of reflection and concentration) used where they occur for the first time and it is an open question, demanding further research whether not only in the Bhagavadgita but also throughout the Mahabharata, the words Sankhya and Yoga are not so much names of philosophical systems as general terms for the two methods of reflection and concentration."

CHAPTER ONE

Karma Yoga

Definition

The Yoga which we shall consider first of all will be Karma Yoga. "Karma" is a Sanskrit word derived from the root "Kri" to do, and the primary meaning of the word therefore is action. There are other secondary significance of the word, but in Karma – Yoga, it is action that is the subject of enquiry. Action considered as due from us some one else is known as duty. Action performed in accordance with Sastraic injunctions is a ritual. Karma- Yoga embraces all these phases of action, and it is the science which treats of not only actions but also their motives and tendencies as well as the results.

Escape from Work impossible

The Gita recognises that work is the order of nature, man is incessantly changing, animals are changing, plants are changing and even minerals are changing. Not a single second passes without producing enormous changes in nature, in the mineral, vegetable and animal kingdoms. The whole of nature is as it were a workshop of uninterrupted business. Nature knows no rest and is identical with ever-recurring work. Knowingly or unknowingly every being from a blade of grass to the highest angel is working. Now, this repeating work or change is brought about by three fundamental forces according to the Sankhya philosophers. They call them *Gunas.* The three Gunas are Sattwam, Rajas and Tamas.[1] The English word "forces" does not fully express the original idea, for Gunas are not forces as opposed to matter but are themselves the constituents of primordial matter out of which the whole of creation is evolved according to the Sankhya philosophy. The translation "quality" is open to a similar objection. So far as action is concerned we may translate Sattwam as the *equalizing,* Rajas as the *differentiating,* and Tamas as the *deadening* force. Nature is the field of competition among these fundamental forces. Thus, on one side we see the Sattwa force working to bring out harmony and equilibrium, on another, there is the Rajas predominant, showing enormous activity and giving room to numerous inequalities, while in the third place there is the Tamas stopping all action and producing nothing but inertness. These forces are at work everywhere. "न तदस्ति पृथिव्यां वा दिवि देवेषु वा पुनः। सत्त्वं प्रकृतिजैर्मुक्तं यदेभिः स्यात्त्रिभिर्गुणैः॥XVIII.40॥ ." There is no being on the surface of the earth or even among the Gods of Heaven, who is free from these fundamental Gunas of nature. Now, it is part of the province of Karma Yoga to study the working of these forces and their effect on human character.

As said above, everyone has to work.

"न हि कश्चित्क्षणमपि जातु तिष्ठत्यकर्मकृत्।
कार्यते ह्यवशः कर्म सर्वः प्रकृतिजैर्गुणैः॥3.5॥"

" No one indeed ever stands without work even for a moment; every one is forced to work, in spite of himself, by the Gunas of nature." Whether we will or no, we have to march. If any one stops even for a single second, striking work, he is crushed. Man is bound to work and reap the fruits thereof. How rigorous are the laws of nature! There is not the slightest action of the body or of the mind which is not followed by reaction. Every one is working either towards equilibrium or differentiation, though for a time if he so chooses, he may also be lazy. Nevertheless, we reap the effects of laziness as well as of work. There is no escape. We may fret and fume, but there is no help for it. We may try to forget this law of nature, we may sleep for a while, we may even take drugs or other soporific thing to make us oblivious of the fact; but after all a hard knock comes and we are forced to recognise the truth, "लोकोऽयं कर्मबन्धनः"[2] "The whole world is bound by its acts (III-9)." Now, Karma Yoga teaches that the sooner we realize this, the better for us. There is no use putting off a question which one day or other, we shall be forced to answer. So, our first duty must be to understand our real position, that we are all forced to work by nature "So long as one has a body, it is impossible to give up works absolutely (XVIII- 10).[3]"

Freedom from Work lies through Work

Nevertheless, man is ever struggling for freedom. This is also a fact. On the one hand, Nature is forcing man to be her slave; on the other, man is fiercely fighting against her, with a deep-rooted conviction that he is sure to be the master in the end. If there is any ingrained belief in us all alike, it is the idea of freedom. If Nature is trying to put limitations after limitations to man's power, man is trying to transcend all such limitations if possible. Nature wants man incessantly to work and at the same time man's heart yearns for rest. The wheel of action is turning round incessantly and man is being carried on with it. Yet he wants complete rest and complete freedom.

Is this struggle of man in vein or is there any hope? This is a very important question. For, on the answer to this question depends the foundation of morality. If man is a mere creature of circumstances, and is forced to drudge in spite of himself, if he is no more than a wind-bound vessel in the ocean of life, his responsibility ceases, and he can neither be blamed for his evil actions nor be given credit for virtuous deeds. If, on the other hand, he is a master of his actions to any extent, and not a slave of the forces of Nature, there is hope for ethics. Man himself becomes directly responsible for his actions to the extent of his liberty. So, this question has to be put and answered. Is man free to work or is he forced to work? The Gita says, man as he is, must work in spite of himself, but it lies with him to choose the line of work. He may take a rope and hang himself or use the same rope by himself to bind elephants and tigers and rule them. He may work out his own ruin or salvation. "One is one's own friend and one's own foe. उद्धरेदात्मनाऽऽत्मानं नात्मानमवसादयेत्। आत्मैव ह्यात्मनो बन्धुरात्मैव रिपुरात्मन:।।6.5।।*" To teach how to turn work to advantage and how to work out one's own salvation is the special aim of Karma Yoga.*

So then, the Gita admits that freedom is desirable and possible. But it says that this freedom lies through work and not through inaction "not by non-commencement of works alone does a person get freedom of works alone does a person get freedom of action, nor can he by mere abandonment of works attain perfection न कर्मणामनारम्भान्नैष्कर्म्यं पुरुषोऽश्नुते न च संन्यसनादेव सिद्धिं समधिगच्छति।। III.4 ।। " Victory is to be won not by deserting your post, but by bravely fighting where you are. If you want rest, you must find it in work or nowhere. Why not find rest throwing all actions overboars? Simply because it is impossible to do so while you live. Cessation of work means cessation of life. "Life itself would be impossible without work." नियतं कुरु कर्म त्वं कर्म ज्यायो ह्यकर्मण:। शरीरयात्रापि च ते न प्रसिद्ध्येदकर्मण:।। III.8 ।। " For, what is life but a struggle with nature? So, this struggle is to go on to the end of life. Saints and sinners, rich and poor, young and old, all alike are subject to this struggle. Our choice therefore lies not between work and no work, but netween drudgery and intelligent work, between working like a slalve of nature, and working like a master. Karma Yoga teaches us the art of intelligent work.

Two kinds of Works

दूरेण ह्यवरं कर्म बुद्धियोगाद्धनञ्जय। बुद्धौ शरणमन्वच्छि कृपणाः फलहेतवः॥2.49॥
"Far removed is lower Karma (work) from the Yoga of intelligent work, Oh! Wealth winner; seek refuge in this wisdom, for pitiable are those that are led by desire of rewards. (II- 49)" Here Sri Krishna wanted to emphasize the distinction between these two kinds of works, the work of a slave and the work of a master. But the laconical manner in which this is stated in the second chapter of the Gita and the concluding verses of that chapter which describe the wisdom of a Yogin without special reference to work gave room to Arjuna's question with which the third chapter opens, "If, Oh! Janardana, you hold wisdom to be greater than work, then why do you press me to take part in this terrific war? (III − 1)[4]" Evidently Arjuna takes it that there is meant here a natural antithesis between wisdom and work, whereas the real contrast intended to be specially brought home is between lower Karma "अवर कर्म " and higher intelligent Karma "बुद्धि योग | " [5] The whole of the third and a great deal of the fourth chapter is devoted to make this point clear. Sri Krishna points out that while it is true that there are two paths of realization called Jnana Yoga and Karma Yoga suited to different temperaments, yet they are not mutually exclusive, nor is it true that Jnana means cessation from all work, for as already shown it is physically impossible. The only thing to be noticed and remembered is that whereas ordinary mortals like servants, the Karma Yogin works like a master. The three forces of nature , Sattwam, Rajas and Tamas already referred to have no control over him; for he has learnt to manipulate them without coming under their influence.

Three Gunas or Fundamental forces of Nature

A knowledge of the working of these three forces is absolutely necessary for one wishing to be a Karma Yogin. A general description of them is given in the fourteenth chapter and again in the eighteenth. We shall here give the translation of three of these Slokas (XIV – 5 to 8). "Sattwam, Rajas and Tamas – the three manifest Gunas oof nature bind the embodied undecaying soul. Of these, Oh! Spotless Arjuna, Sattwam being pure is enlightening and purifying; it binds one with attachment to happiness as well as with attachment to knowledge. Know Rajas to be passion, the birth – place of vehement desire and fondness; it binds the embodied being with attachment to activity. As for Tamas, know it to be born of ignorance and stupefying to all embodied beings; it binds them with negligence, indolence and drowsiness." Thus there is constantly going on this interaction of the triple nature. Every act of ours is goaded on by one of these forces. It must not be supposed, however, that these forces work singly each in its special field. They are simultaneously at play and mixed in different combinations produce different effects on the agents. One of these forces may be predominant in an individual, and that may determine his choice of work. His choice and action again will have special reaction and effect on himself as well as on his surroundings.

.

Work without Attachment

The Chief Doctrine of Karma Yoga

Now, Karma Yoga teaches that work by itself is quite harmless and all our miseries come from our *Sanga* (attachment) to the work done by the three Gunas. "Persons ignorant of the Gunas of nature, get attached to their actions. (III- 29)[6] ." If we just understand this a right and avoid this error, work becomes a mere play to us, instead of being a bugbear. What is this *Sanga*? It is I-ness. It is a fact observed every where that the best work was produced when the doer forgot *himself,* or rather was wholly engrossed in the work as not to conceive that he was working. Yet people constantly make this mistake of keeping their little personality vividly before their mind and thus spoil the whole work. The instant the idea of "I" comes, we lose sight of our work. As an aid to this practice of non-attachment, and as another factor in making ourselves masters of our actions, the Gita recommends that we should renounce the fruits of work also. It is only when we work without attachment and without desire for fruit that we can become real Karma Yogin. "But my verdict in this matter is this, Oh' Partha, these Karmas ought to be done without attachment and without desire of reward (XVIII – 6).[7]"

This simple doctrine of "action without attachment" seems to have offered unexpected difficulties in certain quarters. The Gita inculcates it as the one key to success in life and containing all the essentials of ethics. Yet certain critics are disposed to think that it is the most poisonous doctrine in the book.

The Rev. J. Lazarus, B.A., for instance, thus comments on the doctrine, "To act without attachment is to act without motive or purpose, to experience in the act itself neither pain nor pleasure, and to thimk noting whatever of its future fruit or result. Action, then, without the three concomitants of motive, feeling and effect is action without attachment. Men are to be mere animals or living automate, acting as they are moved by instinct. The moment that any one of these attachments is formed the actions become sinful. For a rational being such as man is, it is utterly impossible to act without attachment so called unless he becomes mad or delirious. The moral element, not to speak of the physical, would be utterly wanting in it; no such action would be possible. How was Arjuna as a human being and a kinsman to dismiss all feelings of pity and mercy for the foes against whom he was aiming his deadly darts? Action without attachment is a convenient loop-hole for the commission of any crime however horrible or foul. The murderer of Mr. Rand walked up to the gallows with the Gita in his hand. I am afraid this is the most poisonous doctrine in the book."[8] (Vide Lectures on the Bhagavadgita, by Rev. J. Lazarus, pp. 11,12).

Now, one peculiar feature of this extraordinary piece of criticism is that it takes immense pains to father upon the author of the Gita a doctrine which he never taught and then passes the severe judgment on the Gita that it propounds a "Poisonous" doctrine. We have therefore only to explain the real doctrine in order to show that the criticism stands self-refuted. Action without attachment does not mean "to act without motive or purpose and to think nothing whatever of its future fruit or result." Action without any motive is a physical impossibility even for a mad man, for even he has some fancied motive for his conduct. All actions is *motion* and as such necessarily requires a *motive*. Even inaction is, strangely enough, due to some motive. This the Gita recognises fully and says that in this sense, inaction may be also spoken of as a species of action (IV-18). By action without attachment again, is never meant an action without feeling. For man, as he is, is a bundle of feelings and every action is sure to bring about a necessary feeling in the agent. Thus to touch fire and not to expect a feeling of burning sesation would be possible only for the most obtuse-minded person. Nor does action without attachment mean "thinking nothing whatever of its future fruit of effect." Though such an action is possible, none but would stoop to it. What the Gita has to say on an action without any concern for results will be clear from the following: "Regardless of its future effects, of what it costs, of the trouble it involves and of the capacity required for its execution – an action undertaken without regard to any of these is said to be Tamasic (of the lowest type) XVIII - 25[9]. The best action on the other hand , is described in the Gita in the following words: "That action which, as a rule, is done without attachment , which is the outcome of neither love nor hatred, and which is performed with a view to no personal gain, is said to be Satwic (of the best type) XVIII – 23.[10] " Karma Yoga therefore does not ask us to become mere animal and to act as we are "moved by the instinct." It does not mean an action "without the three concomitants of motive, feeling and effect." It only asks us to have the highest of motives, the best of feelings and always to undertake actions calculated to bring about the greatest amount of good while it costs the least trouble either to ourselves or to others.

The reader will have by this time pretty clearly understood what is meant by the expression "सङ्गरहति कर्म " "action without attachment." Being acted upon by the three fundamental Gunas afore-mentioned, man has the curious knack of attaching himself to their acts and as it were becoming a mere appendage to them. He says to himself "I am doing this, this is to be done by me now." (XVI -13). The moment this thought occurs in his mind, this *Ahankara* or egoistic tendency destroys much of his energy. According to the Gita, there is a higher mood in which man can place himself and in which alone his actions are at their best. All the great men of the world have consciously or unconsciously put themselves in this mood when they achieved the greatest of their performances. Now, the Gita says that it is the *Sanga* or the clinging to the "I" that obstructs our passing to this mood. If we are consciously to get this higher state, we have to give up this clinging to our little self; in plain words we are to give up selflessness. This doctrine is the very basis of Hindu or for that matter universal ethics. All ethics preaches nothing but the destruction of this lower "I." The lower self or *Ahankara* is to be destroyed; this is the one theme of all religion. Till this lower self is gone, there is no hope of the higher being attained. As the poet says ---

"Unless above himself he can

Erect himself, how mean a thing is man!"

And what is "फलत्याग:" Renunciation of fruits? It is not to be regardless of the consequences of an action, but to forget our individual gain or loss, nor to think of what return we are to get for the deed. We are required to see that our energies are not frittered away by thinking of little temporary gains. For, it is only action done by a man expecting no personal gain that is calculated to produce a lasting effect. It is this renunciation of fruit, for instance, that displayed itself in the founders of all religions. Had they thought of the fruit or the result to accrue to themselves by their actions, they would have never become great men and their names would have been buried in oblivion like those of a thousand other persons.

Thus the doctrine of "giving up attachment and fruit of action" is neither impossible nor absurd. It is not meant for mad and delirious persons but for brave souls who can work for the good of the world without expecting any reward. There is thus no "want" or absence of the moral or any other element in actions without attachment and without desire for fruit, for only in such actions do morality and physical energy find the widest field for their fullest play.

But it must be borne in mind that the Gita does not depreciate other actions, for , according to this book, even selfish actions are not necessarily sinful. Though unselfish action ought to be the goal, yet it is not possible for us all. So, we may work with selfish motives if we cannot help it. Indeed to work with some motive (including a selfish one) is preferable to indolence. "Work is better than no work." (III – 8). To give up laziness, the first step is to take up some work. A great many of us find it impossible to go beyond this stage. We are doing some work, with some motive. Some are working for money, and they would not be content even were they to amass the wealth of *Kubera* himself. Even if a portion of this wealth should be diminished by chance they would break their heart over it, like that millionaire of Rome who, finding one day that he had only a million pounds left, is said to have died in intense sorrow. Then there are those who work for power. In their eyes nothing is all right unless it has power. Even God Himself is no God if He is not All powerful. They set value on things in terms of power. Thus, "knowledge is power, money is power, time is power." Knowledge, money and time are valuable to them only as conducing to power. So, they work for power. But others work for knowledge. They are quite dissatisfied with those who work for any other ideal. How beautiful, how excellent is knowledge! All money , all power is nothing before knowledge. Others again work for name, fame and honour. There are various other motives too numerous to mention. Suffice it to say that the Gita condemns none. No work done with one, or even more selfish motives is sinful in itself. You may work for enjoyment either here or hereafter, the Gita has no quarrel with you. Avoid inaction by all means . "Always work (III- 8) [11]" that is all it has to say.

But a rational being should eventually see that there are higher motives also. To work for wealth, power or fame is good, but to work because it is our duty to work is better. To work because it does good to the world is still higher stage. To work for the sake of work is a yet higher motive; to work not because it brings us enjoyment, not because it is our duty to some one else, not because we wish to do good to the world and to imrove it, but because intelligent good work is in itself an ideal, is the highest stage that man can reach in the present world. To be always doing good and to be always loving good is in itself a state of blessedness for which no other enjoyment can be a match. To taste of this eternal fountain of joy, discovered by never-ceasing and selfish work is the highest of motives with which man can be actuated.

A word more is necessary about another "concomitant of action" as it has been aptly termed by our Reverend critic. We have now fairly done with motive and effect of actions; there remains "feeling." By what feeling are we to be actuated in our actions? The definition of Satwic karma already quoted says "अरागद्वेष त: कृतम." Our work must not be the result of love or hatred. Very often we imagine that unless we are excited by some passion we cannot work. It is true that feeling is a necessary concomitant of work, but it does not necessarily follow that we should feel the passions as vehemently as we do generally. Indeed our feelings spoil the work rather than help it. The one feeling that we should possess is unruffled calmness. It is only when the mind is very calm and collected that it can accomplish anything great. Hence it is that the Gita says, "Do your actions, taking stand in Yoga, giving up all attachment, being undisturbed in mind, either by success or failure. (II – 48)[12]" And what is this Yoga in which we should place ourselves. "Evenness is called Yoga."

This evenness, this equipoise of mind, is the higher mood in which every one should try to place himself while at work. It is not the man given to love or hatred or anger or any other passion that can do real and useful work, but only a person who commands a calm and well balanced mind.[13] This evenness or undisturbed balance of mind is the secret of success. A man swayed by passion is always in a hurry, for, before he has in one mood determined what to do, he is carried away by another passion. How can masterly work be possible to one who is ever a slave to his passion? On the other hand, "a mind can well weigh its motives and tendencies. It can think rightly, determine rightly and choose rightly. "Therefore apply yourself to this Yoga, for, in action Yoga (balance of mind) is the skill.(II – 50)[14]" [15]All clever and intelligent work is the outcome of this balance of mind.

The Gita on Duty

Now, it becomes easy to understand why Krishna calls Arjuna a coward when he refuses to fight. "Whence at this juncture comes upon thee, Oh , Arjuna, this despair, un-Aryan, disgraceful and obstructing the heavenward path! Yield not to cowardice, Oh! PArtha, it doth not become thee; cast off this mean weakness of the heart, and arise, Oh! Vexer of thy foes." (II -2). Arjuna as a human being and a kinsman, naturally felt for his foes. He was,as any other ordinary mortal would have been, overwhelmed with mercy and pity for them and refused to fight. But this was just the time when he ought not to have sold himself to these passions. He came to fight and goaded by his warrior spirit was sure to fight, but meanwhile came this weakness of heart in the grab of pity and love for his kinsmen. Thus he was first subject to a heroic passion and then to the passion of pity and worldly love and in a moment more, perhaps he would have changes his mind again, and reminded of the wrongs done to him and his brothers by those enemies, he would have certainly made ready to aim his deadly darts at them. This is what Sri Krishna warned him against. " You think egoistically that you are not going to fight, but this determination will be in vein, for your inborn spirit will compel you(to fight); nature-bidden and predestined by your own action, that which you do not relish to do(now), you will do in spite of yourself. (XVIII – 59-60)[16]" This giving way to the passion and to be readily acted on by feelings as they come, is what is rightly denounced as cowardice by Sri Krishna. Instead of fighting like a hero, Arjuna chose to fight like a slave spurred on by passion. This was the true situation of Arjuna though he declared to the contrary. From a prudential point of view, it was a decided loss to him not to fight, for, he was losing one of the rarest opportunities, which being embraced would lead him on to fortune, fame and honour. From a moral point of view, he was shrinking his duty as a king, for it was his duty as well as his interest to enter into a righteous war but for which a great calamity would have befallen his country. The war between Pandavas and Kauravas was no mere party strife but really a fight between right and wrong. By giving up this purely on sentimental grounds, therefore, Arjuna was committing a great moral blunder, (II- 33). Looking at from the standpoint of philosophy, Arjuna's refusal to fight amounted to a spiritual self-degradation. It was nothing short of limiting the One Infinite, Unborn, and Undecaying Atman. Arjuna was in fact immersed in sorrow for want of real Vedantic knowledge. A truly enlightened person neither avoids a piece of work as bad nor unnecessarily courts another thinking it good, (XVIII – 10) but his own balance of mind by thinking of its consequences to him. But Arjuna immersed in sorrow has no time to think over such matters. Sri Krishna therefore considers Arjuna a coward. Arjuna according to Krishna is a coward not because he refuses to fight but because he yields to passion, because he is committing a moral sin by giving up his duty, and finally because he does not know and has not the courage to face the truth of philosophy and religion, though he argues all the same like one well-versed in both.

Thus the Gita does not propound a philosophy of fighting, as has been erroneously thought by some superficial students. Nor does it support in any way the commission of heinous crimes as has been insinuated by persons who do not know what they say. The Karma Yoga of the Gita instructs us not to be over-ridden by passion, not to give up the duties next to us, nay more, to rise even above the idea of duty if possible and to work in a calm and undisturbed manner. In whatever sphere of life we may be, we are to learn to work without passion, faithfully and disinterestedly to discharge our duties, and to work for work's sake. The refrain "therefore fight" found in various places of the Gita in various forms of expression if interpreted in this spirit, justifies the claim of the Gita as a guide in practical life. To a lover of peace no less than to a lover of righteous war, to the poor no less than to the rich, to the subject no less than to the King, the Gita offers this one piece of advice: "In whatever station of life you may be placed, do your duty not like a slave but like a hero." Perfection is possible for all in this way alone. " Engaged in his own duty man attains perfection. (XVIII – 45)[17]. " How are we to know our duty? The Gita says "The sastras are your authority in determining what is or is not duty. (XVII – 24)[18]" WE are not to depend on mere speculation in this matter , for, if we do, there will be no end to our doubts. What is considered right in one country and at a particular time, becomes wrong in another country at another time. Different ideas, indeed, of right and wrong prevail among men even of the same country and time, and men placed in the same condition. The ethics of any individual or society therefore, represents the degree of perfection to which that individual or society has developed its conscience. But it may be contended, does it not follow, for this very reason morality should depend upon conscience and not upon scripture or authority? The answer is that it does follow. The Gita does not recommend any atrophy of the conscience, but only teaches that we should be guided by a sense of duty rather than of interest. Self-interest understood in the highest sense of the word; does not really clash with a sense of duty (VII – 11). But in the limited sphere in which interest usually functions in most of us, it will be necessary to be cautioned against it. When left to himself, man is apt to choose the temporarily pleasurable to what is eventually and eternally beneficial to him. But if instead of his personal speculation, he submits himself to the guidance of Scripture, which is only another name for exert opinion; he is not likely to go wrong. Many of us have not the presence of mind to choose the right even if it should go in the teeth of our interest. Hence the Gita says, "He who rejects the injunctions of ethical science and acts ever impelled by desires he never attain perfection, he gets to neither happiness, nor the highest goal. (XVII – 23).[19] "

Now the ethical demands of any particular time depend as remarked above, on the degree of perfection which conscience has attained, and therefore ethical science can only indicate the general lines of conduct, while the particulars will have always to be worked according to the needs of the time. For instance, at the time of the Gita, caste was a well-ordered institution, and the author of the Gita therefore, very often applies the general laws of ethics to caste, just to show their practical bearing on life. But though caste confusion has more or less taken place in India in own times, the Gita not only continues to take a hold on the minds of the Hindus, but influences non-Hindus also to a great extent. This suffices to show that the basement of the vast superstructure of the ethics of the Gita is not caste, as has been alleged by some. Its teachings are general enough to be applicable to any society whether with or without caste. The teachings of Karma Yoga, in particular, admit of application today as were thousands of years ago.

Principle of Conduct

The most important principle of conduct required by Karma Yoga

Though we have already alluded to the general principles of conduct recommended by Karma Yoga, we shall now state the most important of them in brief. "Except in the case of an action done for the sake of sacrifice, the world is action-bound; for that(sacrifice) do thou, Oh! Son of Kunti, perform action. (III – 9)[20]. " This is the first principle of work. But for sacrifice, we become bound to our actions. What is sacrifice? Several kinds of sacrifices are spoken of in the Gita (Ch IV) "sacrifice to the Gods, sacrifice though concentration, sacrifice through study and knowledge." The one idea that pervades all these is killing selfishness. The idea of Me and Mine which vitiates our life is to be removed. It is difficult to enumerate all actions which are always right, but as a general rule it may be said, that which tends to unselfishness is right, while that which makes us selfish is wrong. Though the world is bound through work, self-sacrifice cuts through the bonds of Karma. Indeed, Karma becomes no Karma- in so far its evil effects are concerned – to a person of self- sacrifice. " For him who works for sacrifice, all actions disappears (in its evil aspects). (IV – 23)[21]." Self-sacrifice is the first principle of conduct.

The second principle is cheerfulness. " Every sense organ has its established love or hatred towards sense-objects; but one should not yield to these (passions); for, they are his foes (III -34)[22] ." we have already dwelt upon this principle at length; a person should not be guided by strong passions in his actions, for, the more he can dissociate himself from passions and assume a calm attitude, the greater will be the success he can attain.

The third principle is Faithful discharge of guty. "better is one's own duty though lacking in some quality, than another's duty well performed; better face death is one's own duty, for, another's duty is full of danger.(III – 35)[23]" It has been already remarked that the Gita often applies principles of ethics to caste. One of the objects of Sri Krishna was to show that Arjuna was wrong in proposing to give up his duty as a Kshatriya. Some persons misunderstand this teaching and are willing to make friends with the context, can see that the real point at issue is not caste but duty dependent upon birth and position in life.[24] We are apt to see others through our own eyes and to judge all customs by our own standpoint. The main teaching of the Gita on duty is intended to show that this is an error. Though duty as a general idea exists in all our minds, we see that duty as manifested in life changes with environments. Karma Yoga requires us all to be cheerful in discharging our duty by birth as well as those by our position in life.[25] If one satisfactorily erforms his own duties however humble, nature selects him for higher duties. We should not neglect our own duty imagining that we are better qualified to do another duty. We are to show our fitness to higher duties by the proper discharge of our duty in the position we are placed in.

The fourth principle of Karma Yoga is that we should keep ourselves enlightened with knowledge so as not to be deceived by the three forces of nature. "But the knowledge of the real nature of distinguishing Gunas and their works, Oh strong-armed Arjuna, thinks that it is only Gunas acting on Gunas is therefore unattached (III -28)[26] ." The Gunas have been treated of already. A true knowledge of the several ways in which they work enables us to be out of their trammels. Thieves break into only an ungrounded house. While we keep the light of truth, we cannot be taken in by the Gunas. Sri Krishna therefore advises Arjuna thus " The Vedas are for those who are attached to the three Gunas; free from oposites, ever taking stand in Satwa, be free from a sense of possessing everything, and be self-controlled (II – 45)[27] ." Of the three Gunas, the influence of Tamas is to be overcome by Rajas, and Rajas with the aid of Satwam, for, while, one Guna is predominant, the other two are necessarily powerless (XIV – 10). When one learns the habit of being always in Satwam, he gets gradually beyond all three, for it has to be noticed here that pure Satwam is quite different in its effects from the Satwam mixed with Rajas and Tamas. It is for this reason tthat one who ever engaged himself in purely Satwic Actions, is said to be a "Trigunateetah (त्ररगि्णातीत:) " (one who has got beyond the influence of the three Gunas). A description of such an ideal person is given at the conclusion of the fourteenth chapter.

From the advice that one should go beyond all the three Gunas and then take one's stand in Satwam, another principle can be inferred and deserves to be noted here. As shown above we have to shake ourselves off Tamas and Rajas before we get to the ure Satwam, all the seeds of evil such as Kama and Krodha being the outcomes of Rajas

काम एष क्रोध एष रजोगुणसमुद्भव:।

महाशनो महापाप्मा वद्धियेनेमहि वैरिणम्॥ III.37॥.

This is in effect the same as saying that even if we cannot do good deeds all at ones, our first duty must be to give up bad ones. This is expressly taught in the Satasamhita by saying "अकुर्वन्नपि वधियिक्रुतन नषिद्धिन् परविर्जयेत्" (though one cannot fulfil the duty enjoined in S;astras, one should give up the prohibited act.) In the Gita also Sri Krishna says to

Arjuna:

तस्मात्त्वमिन्द्रियाण्यादौ नियम्य भरतर्षभ।

पाप्मानं प्रजहि ह्येनं ज्ञानविज्ञाननाशनम्।। III.41।।

"Therefore Oh best of the descendants of Bharata, kill first of all this sinful (enemy born of Rajas) destroyer of knowledge and realisation, having controlled the senses." The application of this principle is very simple. It only requires us, for instance, to desist at least from hurling vindictive language against a poor beggar even if we do not give him any alms.

Meekness of spirit is the next principle of Karma Yoga:

कायेन मनसा बुद्ध्या केवलैरिन्द्रियैरपि।

योगिनः कर्म कुर्वन्ति सङ्गं त्यक्त्वाऽऽत्मशुद्धये।। V.11।।

" Through body, mind, and even by the senses, Yogin work giving up attachment for the sake f self purity." There is great spiritual danger in thinking that the world is in need oof our help. In spite of our working, the world will always be the same on the whole. The world in fact neither makes towards infinite progress nor is it going awfully backwards. It will be just where it is, and will go on without us. To think that the world is bad and is waiting for our help is absurd. God has created it for a purpose and it is perfectly well adapted for that purpose. It does in no way stand in need of us. But we should think it privilege to be allowed to work here. Our unselfish work eventually hels us most. It is for "आत्म शुद्धिः" self-purification, rather than for the good of the world that we work. This meekness of spirit is an important principle of Karma Yoga.

We now come to the last though by no means the least important principle of Karma Yoga. "How are we to be self-less? How are we to free ourselves from assions? How are we to discharge our duty without attachment? How are we to rise above the pride that we are helping others while we do the right?" it is indeed very hard to do all these. Unless we have a method to pursue in this respect, Karma Yoga will be a nere talk. Now, those that do not believe in God are left to themselves. They have somehow to get at this ideal. By sheer force of their will, they have to rise above all actions and become free. They have no other resource except their determination to get unattached. A person who asks "How can I do it?" already confesses ignorance as well as weakness, and a willingness likewise to be instructed and guided. To such person, Karma Yga offers the method of renunciation of work to God. Sri Krishna says to Arjuna

मयि सर्वाणि कर्माणि संन्यस्याध्यात्मचेतसा।

निराशीर्नर्ममो भूत्वा यध्ध्यस्व वगितज्वर:।। III.30।।

"Having renounced all work unto Me with a holy mind – without desires and without the idea of mine, fight thou, freed from sorrow." Giving up all works unto God is the safest method. All our duties are really His. We are all doing His will here. We are merely His instruments, and all fruits of action go to Him. Ours is only to serve. Let us try to do the duty allotted to us as best as we can, but let us claim no praise for it. For, it is all Good's. This renunciation of the lower self to God must go on ceaselessly till we get into habit of doing so unconsciously. "Whatever one does by nature in deed, word, mind, senses or intellect, all that must be given us to the great Lord." This self –renunciation to the Lord makes us free. The idea of duty will no longer be a bugbear of life, but it will be the leasantest cause to do the bidding of the Lord.

यत: प्रवृत्तिर्भूतानां येन सर्वमिदं ततम्।

स्वकर्मणा तमभ्यर्च्य सिद्धिं विन्दति मानव:।।18.46।।

"Worshipping God with his duty, man attains perfection." We work not because it is our duty to work, but because it is our privilege to work. We are noto slaves to duty, but free servants of the Lord. Never thinking either of rewards or punishments, we work out His will. This constant thinking of God is the secret of non-attachment.

मच्चित्त: सर्वदुर्गाणि मत्प्रसादात्तरिष्यसि।

अथ चेत्त्वमहङ्कारान्न श्रोष्यसि विनङ्क्ष्यसि।। XVIII.58।।

"Minded in Me, you can surmount all difficulties"[28] says Sri Krishna.

Such are the general principles of Karma Yoga. This Yoga solves the problem of life through self-less work. The true Karma Yogin does not shrink work, for, he has realised the most important truth that intense self-less work is the real rest and that mere laziness of wilful giving up of work is really work that binds the soul.

कर्मण्यकर्म य: पश्येदकर्मणि च कर्म य:।

स बुद्धिमान् मनुष्येषु स युक्त: कृत्स्नकर्मकृत्।। IV.18।।

True rest, true actlessness is to work always disinterestedly for the good of the world. Real rest, indeed, does not depend upon working or not working. It is merely a certain state of the mind. Eternal rest is attainable only by those that have reached the true Yoga of "Evenness of mind." He who can be busy always and yet can enjoy such complete rest is the ideal Karma Yogin.

[1] *Though the terminology of the Sankhya philosophy (Sattwam, Rajas, Tamas, Prakruti etc.) is used throughout the Gita, the work it will be seen is pre-eminently Vedantic. This process of making Vedanta a superstructure on the Sankhya phraseology is by no means uncommon in religio-philosophic writings. Moreover no terminology can be considered peculiarly Vedantic or Sankhyaic as is sometimes done.*

[2] यज्ञार्थात्कर्मणोऽन्यत्र लोकोऽयं कर्मबन्धनः।
तदर्थं कर्म कौन्तेय मुक्तसंगः समाचर॥ III.9 ॥

[3] न द्वेष्ट्यकुशलं कर्म कुशले नानुषज्जते।
त्यागी सत्त्वसमाविष्टो मेधावी छिन्नसंशयः॥ XVIII.10 ॥

[4] ज्यायसी चेत्कर्मणस्ते मता बुद्धिर्जनार्दन।
तत्किं कर्मणि घोरे मां नियोजयसि केशव॥3.1॥

[5] *Sankara's commentary on the above where* "बुद्धि योगात्" *is interpreted as* "बुद्धि युक्तात्".

[6] प्रकृतेर्गुणसम्मूढाः सज्जन्ते गुणकर्मसु।
तानकृत्स्नविदो मन्दान्कृत्स्नविन्न विचालयेत्॥3.29॥

[7] एतान्यपि तु कर्माणि सङ्गं त्यक्त्वा फलानि च।
कर्तव्यानीति मे पार्थ निश्चितं मतमुत्तमम्॥18.6॥

[8] *What a strange piece of argument is this, to infer from the sinful action of a murderer that danger lurks in one of the righteous doctrine inculcated in the Gita, a most well-known ethical work, and to make it responsible for heinous crimes! if this book really supported crimes, the millions of people in India that reverently read it every day, should have by this time sunk to the lowest depths of immorality. But as Miss E. Waldo says, "In the statistics of crime for the whole civilized world, the percentage of India is the lowest. The high system of ethics that has been inculcated there for ages has its effects and today it is still manifest." How the Gita provides the surest foundation of morality so well recognized by Western scholars like Dr. Paul Deussen, will become clear from the concluding remarks of this book.*

[9] अनुबन्धं क्षयं हिंसामनपेक्ष्य च पौरुषम्।
मोहादारभ्यते कर्म यत्तत्तामसमुच्यते॥18.25॥

[10] नियतं सङ्गरहितमरागद्वेषतः कृतम्।
अफलप्रेप्सुना कर्म यत्तत्सात्त्विकमुच्यते॥18.23॥

[11] नियतं कुरु कर्म त्वं कर्म ज्यायो ह्यकर्मणः।
शरीरयात्रापि च ते न प्रसिद्ध्येदकर्मणः॥3.8॥

[12] योगस्थः कुरु कर्माणि सङ्गं त्यक्त्वा धनञ्जय।

सद्धिध्यसद्धिध्यो: समो भूत्वा समत्व योग उच्यतो।।2.48।।

[13] "Emotions should be servants, not masters; or at least not tyrants. The secret lies in the will. The personality should reside there as in a castle." – Rev. Robert Hugh Benson.

[14] बुद्धयिक्तो जहातीह उभे सुकृतदुष्कृतो
तस्माद्योगाय युज्यस्व योग: कर्मसु कौशलम्।।2.50।।

*[15] "Therefore devote yourself to Yoga. Yoga is success in (all) actions "
(six systems of Philosophy, Prof. Max Muller). This, if taken as defining Yoga as success in all actions, would be against the context.*

[16] यदहङ्कारमाश्रित्य न योत्स्य इति मन्यसो
मथ्यैष व्यवसायस्त प्रकृतिस्त्वा नियोक्ष्यति।। XVIII.59।।
स्वभावजेन कौन्तेय निबद्ध: स्वेन कर्मणा।
कर्तुं नेच्छसि यन्मोहात्करिष्यस्यवशोऽपि तत्।। XVIII.60।।

[17] स्वे स्वे कर्मण्यभिरत: संसद्धिं लभते नर:।
स्वकर्मनरित: सद्धिं यथा वन्दिति तच्छृणु। XVIII.45।।

[18] तस्मादोमित्युद्राहृत्य यज्ञदानतप:क्रिया:।
प्रवर्तन्ते विधानोक्ता: सतत ब्रह्मवादिनाम्।। XVII.24।।

[19] तत्सदिति निर्दिशो ब्रह्मणस्त्रविधि: स्मृत:।
ब्राह्मणास्तेन वेदाश्च यज्ञाश्च विहिता: पुरा।। XVII.23।।

[20] यज्ञार्थात्कर्मणोऽन्यत्र लोकोऽय कर्मबन्धन:।
तदर्थं कर्म कौन्तेय मुक्तसंग: समाचर।। III.9।।

[21] गतसङ्गस्य मुक्तस्य ज्ञानावस्थितिचेतस:।
यज्ञायाचरत: कर्म समग्र प्रविलीयतो। IV.23।।

[22] इन्द्रियस्येन्द्रियस्यार्थे रागद्वेषौ व्यवस्थितौ।
तयोर्न वशमागच्छेत्तौ ह्यस्य परिपन्थिनौ।। III.34।।

[23] श्रेयान्स्वधर्मो विगुण: परधर्मात्स्वनुष्ठितात्।
स्वधर्मे निधन श्रेय: परधर्मो भयावह:।। III.35।।

[24] "The burden of Krishna's teaching is that the zealous performance of his duty is man's most important task to whatever caste he may belong" (page 405, History of Sanskrit Literature by Prof. A, Macdonell)

[25] "We do not choose our own parts in life and have nothing to do with these parts. Our simple duty is confined t playing them well." Epictetus.

[26] तत्त्ववित्तु महाबाहो गुणकर्मविभागयो:।
गुणा गुणेषु वर्तन्त इति मत्वा न सज्जतो। III.28।।

[27] त्रैगुण्यविषया वेदा निस्त्रैगुण्यो भवार्जुन।

नर्द्वन्द्वो नत्यिसत्त्वस्थो नर्ियोगक्षेम आत्मवान्।। II.45।।

[28] This is the connecting link between Karma Yoga and Bhakti Yoga, and as such will be dealt with at length later on when we shall take up Bhakti Yoga

CHAPTER TWO

Dhyana Yoga

What is mysticism? This word is sometimes contemptuously applied to the belief of those that claim to apprehend certain sights and sounds in states called ecstatic and who dogmatically put forth their experiences as the ultimate truth. The word as used here, however, is a synonym for Dhyana[1]. There are many in this world who are of a contemplative turn of mind, who do not much on argument, but are given to constant reflection and brooding till they are convinced of the truth. It is not meant that they never reason or work or do anything else. But self-reflection is their guiding principle of life. They love to examine themselves, to concentrate their mind upon themselves, and to mediate upon what they see in themselves. This method of self –examination and contemplation is known as Dhyana Yoga, or the yoga of mysticism. It is very necessary therefore, to be forewarned that the mysticism here meant has nothing to do with mysteries. Dhyana Yoga should on no account be connected with anything secret. It has no connection whatever, with that branch of speculations which deals with secret-communion or intercourse with angels, spirits or devils or any other imaginary beings. Indeed Dhyana Yoga neither asserts nor denies the existence of such beings or the possibility of human dealings with them. The world of such being is beyond the range of enquiry of Dhyana Yoga. The word mystic in foreign countries is said to denote and include a mind which claims that direct experience of truth is possible and which strives to have such experience. Now, it is in this sense only we call Dhyana Yoga by the name of mysticism, and with reference to the mystery whatever. Yet in a way, Dhyana Yoga may be said to be a Yoga of secret also, Self-examination is, strange to say, a great mystery to the majority of mankind, and while many show inclination and curiosity to know external nature, they live almost in complete ignorance of their own self. For such, therefore, the subject method of Dhyana Yoga will ever remain a supreme secret

"राजगुह्यम" "RAJAGUHYAM." But for all others, who are not satisfied with the surface, but want to probe deeper, the Yoga remains to say the least, an open secret. At all events, nothing secret is ever hinted at in the whole of the Gita.

Reason and Realization

In the consideration of Dhyana Yoga, some persons are confronted in the very beginning with a serious difficulty. These persons are bred into the belief that all knowledge is founded upon reason and therefore naturally ask themselves "I may get to believe or even realize something in a particular state, but where is the proof that what I experience is the truth?" Now, this really an important matter and has to be settled definitely. This is the so-called point of difference between philosophers and mystics. The philosopher thinks that the mystics merely realize without being able to adduce proof, and therefore such knowledge is an assumption at best, till proved: the mystic, on the other hand , wonders how the philosopher can assert that he knows on the mere strength of reasoning. In other to clear up this difficulty, we have to note that all reasoning finally rests on previous experience, for, reason never proceeds except on facts observed and ascertained to be true, and these premises of reasoning are either assumed to be true on the strength of experience or else reasoned from other premises so assumed. Hence even the philosopher must admit that he realize first and then reasons. But this can be no excuse for the mystic, however, to demand others to believe on the strength of his own realization. If he wants to convince others, he must be able to give reasons for his statements when demanded. For, no realization can contradict reasons. The fact is that everyone adopts only one method to ascertain truth – to wit concentration, and when he wants to convince others of his experience, he argues or suggests it in various other ways to them till they take up the suggestion and following the hint are led up to a state where they realize a fact. Hence realisation is the highest proof available and therefore can be no demand there again for a proof. But, realisation is not against reason; it fulfills reason. It covers a waster field than reason but always included reason in its range. The test of true realisation is that the fact realized is under no circumstance contradicted. Again, it must be verifiable by all capable and willing minds. No one can claim special realisation, for which others are eternally disqualified. To be brief, the doctrine of realisation is nothing strange or peculiar. It only assumes that all knowledge is ultimately founded upon universal experience and whatever contradicts such experience is not truth.

Sence pleasure really sources of Misery

Dhyana Yoga as already remarked is the act of attaining that state of fine perception of mind in which it can introspect or look into itself. It is plain that to perform this introspection successfully, one must first cease looking outwards, the majority of people, therefore, are quite unqualified to enter upon this study, since they are ever engaged in extracting pleasure from the outside objects. To help such people, the Gita starts by wanting them against the senses: "All enjoyments arising from the contact of senses and sense-objects are really sources of misery, these (sense – objects) have a beginning and an end, a wise man, therefore does not delight in them (V-22)[2]." This is the great warning of Dhyana Yoga. External nature is really grand and the senses are the gateways of our knowledge of that nature. But what do the senses reveal ? They seem every moment to prove that all external nature is change and quite undeserving of being relied upon. The senses extract all the pleasure they can from the external world and then conclude "This is all we can give you." Even if one is unwise enough to wish to repeat the same monotonous enjoyment of the senses, he is soon disappointed. The senses themselves cannot continue in their vigour forever. The duration of the power of the senses, bears as it were, an inverse ratio to the enjoyment they can give us. Now, this is a sufficient ground for a wise man not to take delight in external enjoyments, which invariably depends upon a particular relation being set up between the self-exhausting senses and the ever changing material nature outside. Thus this pleasure of senses is not only impermanent but also disappointing; being in reality misery is the making in as much as it begets attachment. For, if we get the sense-enjoyment we desire, we become impatient for more and thus make ourselves miserable; but if we do not get the enjoyment, we have to suffer from disappointment. A person who is thus convinced of the utter hollowness of the sense-pleasure, and who is suffering from a mental indigestion of the same for happiness, naturally turns inward to see what he can find there. As the Kathopanishad puts it:

Description: E:\000-02-22-KDP   2022-part   -1\00000-22-kdp-september\000-2210- The Heart\sl-4.bmp

"Outward the self –existence out projected the senses and therefore man looks outward and not within himself. The heroic man only rarely met desiring immortality, with inverted senses examines himself." This wise man who wants to observe and generalise the laws of his internal nature is the person qualified for the pursuit of Dhyana Yoga.

The use of Self Study

What is the use of such study or practice? The best reward for all study is knowledge and there can be no question of utility in the matter. Ignorance is itself a loss which no gain compensates except knowledge. But yet there is utility also here: " One whose mind is unattached to the external sense-pleasure, gets in himself what is (really) happiness; with his mind attached to Brahma Yoga, he gets the highest happiness (V-21) [3]." All misery comes through fear. When we depend upon there is no end to our fears. First there is the fear that the sense-objects, the supposed seats of pleasure, may be themselves destroyed, or they may be lost or else so altered in their nature as to become objects of positive hatred instead of being desirable. There is no depending upon this ever-changing sense – objects. And then the senses themselves are so delusive, they sometimes become diseased and give us false reports of nature or even fail sometimes, to do their proper functions. We can never depend upon these senses, which have developed themselves into their present state almost from being nothing, and they are sure in the long run to lose themselves in nothing. And then the mind! " When the mind is directed to follow the senses, it drives off one's power of judgment, as a wind drives before it a vessel in the waters (II -67)[4]." There can be really no end to the fears and miseries of a man, therefore, who depends upon such a fickle mind, which in its turn depends upon the changing senses and the changing matter, for happiness. At best, happiness to the man of the world means nothing more than avoidance of disappointment and danger. But it is only avoiding <u>Scylla to fall into Charibfies</u>. A worldly man is taken on and on from misery to misery and has no time to enjoy one real happiness. To understand what real happiness consists in, one must turn to himself. The highest bliss is to be attained only when we learn by self-analysis that there is something immortal and perfect in us. Only then can we cease to fear death and to be troubled by vain desires. It is only then that life becomes bearable and even pleasant. This then is the utility of Dhyana Yoga, to point out to us the way of escape from misery and to vouchsafe perfect bliss even in this life.

The need of purification to the Worldly Mind

But the mind in its ordinary state is useless for the pursuit of this Yoga. Thi miind's purity has been dimmed by external dirt. The subtle workings going on in the internal world cannot be reflected in such an opaque mind. Now, man becomes thick-headed mainly through his fault. The Yoga – Vashishtha thus describes the thickening process which a worldling's mind undergoes. "By mistaking the not-self got self, by constant brooding over the body, by an inordinate selfish attachment to life –partner, children and other relations, the mind gets dull. By giving way to the egoistic spirit, by the free play of the dirty idea of "mind" and by constant brooding over things with a sense of exclusive possession, dullness of mind sets in." again the mind has as it were, a natural out-going tendency and therefore finds it comparatively easier to study external nature, but when it has to turn back and study itself, the method becomes extremely difficult. It cannot be made to concentrate on itself, for, it is usually so fickle. Arjuna says in the Gita: " Fickle indeed is the mind, Oh, Krishna, tormenting, strong and firm, I consider its control to be as difficult as that of the wind.(VI -34)[5]" In order to fit the mind therefore for self-study it is necessary not only to subject it , to a thorough cleansing process but also to concentrate its powers till they are thrown on itself. This double process constitutes the chief part of Dhyana Yoga.

Like any other things in nature the human mind usually consists of Satwam, Rajas and Tamas. According to a theory of Dhyana Yoga, the substance of mind in itself is made of pure Satwam, while the Rajas and the Tamas are merely accidents or supports. Rajas is the cause of its restlessness and Tamas makes the mind muddy and dull. As the extraneous Rajas and Tamas are removed, the mind returns more and more to its natural purity and the more Satwic it becomes, the more is it illumined with correct knowledge. Thjs removal of Rajas and Tamas is known as Atma Visuddhi (self-purification) –

The steps in Purification

There are accordingly two steps in the method of this Yoga. First, Tamas has to be overcome, and then Rajas. Rajas being a higher force must be utilized to conquer Tamas and Rajas will have to be controlled by Satwam. The aspirant of the Yoga is called "आरुरुक्षुः" (desirous of ascending) or "आरूढः"(having ascended) according as he is in the first or second stage. In the first stage, the mind is not muddy and not clear; it is inert and has to be roused to action. When it has learnt to be active enough, it is time for it to take to the second step. This is the tranquillising process. "For the sage wishing to ascend the Yoga of Meditation work is the means; to the same person when he has ascended the Yoga, tranquillisation is is said to be the means. [6](VI – 3) "[7]

Karma of the preliminary stage

What are the characteristics of this early training called Karma? All measures taken here should have one object and that is sense-control. To select such actions as will tend to put a check on the ever active senses to keep the intensity of sense – desire and sense – hatred within proper bounds must be our sole aim. We should try to take up the Satwic action described in Karma Yoga. Unless the senses are properly trained in Karma Yoga, it is impossible to control them. It is possible to stop all sense-works but that will be useless, for a mind not qualifies for the higher stage will ever keep thinking of sense –pleasures. "Whosoever restrains the organs of action but keeps thinking of sense – pleasures in his mind, that foolish person is said to be of a hypocritical conduct. But he who mentally restrains his senses and in a spirit of non-attachment undertakes Karma Yoga with the organs of action, is far better (than the other) (III- 6-7)[8]" Work without attachment therefore, must be our rule of conduct at this stage. When by patient striving we attain the second stage, the next method may be taken up.

There is a test which should be applied when the aspirant wants to know, whether he may probably take to the second step, " when one does not get attached t works for the sake of sense – pleasure, and has given up all interested motives, one is said to be a Yogarudha. (VI-4)[9]." It is no doubt a long and difficult process, but unless a person has not under-value sense—pleasures, spiritual life has not begun for him. People often ask for a comfortable religion, a religion that reconciles a life of sensuality with spirituality, but it is only fair to say that there is no such religion. All great teachers have taught that the religious aspirants should never sell himself to the senses. On our moral culture, on our purity, and on our capacity to free ourselves from the power of the senses, depend the attainment of spiritual bliss.

Dhyana Yoga lays down that we ourselves make or mar our life to a great extent. It is not that some malicious and infinitely powerful being has control over us and finds pleasure in subjugating us to the fluctuations of pleasure and pain, but that we in our foolishness make ourselves miserable, "One should raise and should not hurl down himself; for, it is the friend of self and it is the self which is foe to self (VI- 5).[10]" Man would be his own friend, if he controlled himself, and he would be his own enemy if he did not (VI -4). We should, therefore, try to raise ourselves by self-effort, that is by having re-course to Satwic actions, and then we shall have done justice to the self within us. Company of the pious, the reading of books and the hearing of sermons, may quicken the birth of religious yearning in our heart, but the growth of spirituality entirely depends on the individual. A theological objection is sometimes raised against this position by saying that it precludes Divine Mercy be unconditional, it makes the Most supreme being partial. Why should not his Grace descend to the saint and the sinner alike? The idea of Divine Mercy should not be so degraded as to lay the axe at the very root of righteousness. God's Mercy depends entirely on the moral perfection of the soul; for, He has no blood-money. So, even to vindicate God's Mercy we have to admit individual liberty, for, Heaven helps those individual who help themselves. This doctrine of self-help inculcated by the Dhyana Yoga, has the additional advantage of removing all weakness. For, when we are sure that we are the effect of our own past actions and have it in our own power to shape our future, we are never cast down by failure, or disappointments, but learn the glorious lesson of trying to rise every time we fall.

We should therefore prove ourselves our own friends by conquering our self. Self-conquest is the most glorious that can be achieved by man, but it is not to be accomplished by marching cohorts to shed human blood. This must be the harmless war of the spirit against the flesh, the war of our higher nature carried on against our lower nature. When our lower self is finally vanquished, our highest self is gained. This is the greatest gain that can accrue to rational beings. "After gaining which no other gain is considered greater (VI-22).[11]" For, in the words of Jesus, "What is a man profited if he shall gain the world and lose his own soul?"

The second stage of Sama

WHEN BY Satwic conduct, a person has so far conquered himself, as to realize that there is something higher than the sense-plane, he may enter upon the second course of Dhyana Yoga, to "Shamah" or tranquillisation of mind. In all of us thought and action are acting and reacting. Our thoughts influence our acts as much as our acts influence the thoughts. Action is as it were the more concrete and better known of the two, and therefore we first begin by regulating our actions. But this necessarily implies a change in our thoughts, and a man who attends to his actions will soon learn to attend to his thoughts. The study and conscious manipulation of thoughts, is the second step of Dhyana Yoga. It must not be understood that henceforth the student of this Yoga, gives up all actions and converts himself into a recluse, mediator. He only now gives more importance to his mind than to his external behavior. A child first learns to walk and it masters this movement of the body after repeated trials. But it does not give up walking when it has thoroughly learnt it. It performs the movement most gradually but instinctively and now can attend to some other business without caring how it walks. Thus , while a child has to attend a good deal to its mode of walking for fear of falling, the same child as a boy performs that function properly and can afford to devote its thoughts to some higher work. In a similar manner, the Yogin who has learnt to manipulate actions successfully does it almost unconsciously and can without difficulty study the subtler act of thought control.

Renunciation and Practice

The grasping of the mind by itself is a most difficult step to talk. It is something like a pair of tongs trying to turn round and catch itself. Yet this apparently difficult fear has to be performed. The mind has already the power of acting reflexively on itself and this faculty has to be trained and developed. The object of such training must be to make the mind invulnerable. " No doubt, Oh, strong armed Arjuna, the mind is hard of control and restless, but through practice, Oh, son of Kunti, and through dispassion it is conquered (VI-33).[12]" In the first lace practice is absolutely necessary. Religion is not for those who want to have it for mere fashion. The majority of us are content to consider religion as merely one of the accomplishments. We just make a show of religion, - observe certain rites and rituals, say our prayers, read the holy books and then rest satisfied forever. But one who wants to be Dhyana Yogin, should be patient and preserving. He must probe more deeply into himself and be prepared to patiently investigate the self. Mere curiosity will be of no use. A close and constant application is needed. In the second place, freedom from worldly desires is also necessary. Man is being dragged hither and thither by a thousand vain desires, and never knows the clam necessary for self—study. So long as he is not dissatisfied, with the senses, he cannot taste of higher happiness.

What is Renunciation?

This is the place for a little more detailed consideration of renunciation. Two words are used in the Gita. to express this idea: they are "सन्यास:" and " वैराग्यम" . Sanyasa means giving up and Vairagya is desirelessness. There have been a certain order of monks technically called Sanyasis and because of the ascetic like practices of some of them, it has been the custom with some to suppose that the essentials of Sanyasa are ascetism. The word VIRAKTA (dispassionate) likewise has been often misapplied to persons who are averse to the stern duties of life. Now, this strange notion seems to have been as old as the time of the Gita for, the author remarks:

अनाश्रतिः कर्मफल कार्य कर्म करोतयि:।

स संन्यासी च योगी च न नरिग्नरि्न चाक्रयि:।। VI.1।।

"He who does his duty not depending upon results, is the real Sanyasin, is the real Yogin, not the man who is merely without the household fire, nor the man who is given up all work." Now, this Sanyasins, elaborates noyhing more special but only points out what constitutes the essential Sanyasa or renunciation. True renunciation does not depend upon one's position, or rank, it does not depend upon one's food, dress or ways of living. It is nothing more than giving up of selfish acts (XVIII – 2). Vairagya is simply rising above desires. Man, as he is, is hampered by numerous desires which clash against one another. When he rises above them and lets them alone, they will fructify one another leisurely.

In so many places have we spoken of giving up the senses, of freedom from worldly attachment and of rising above worldly desires, that an explanation seems due here. The Dhyana Yoga is not pessimistic. It does not say that the world is a mass of evil. At the same time it is not optimistic, for it does not think that the world is all-sufficient in its present conditions. The world is according to this view neither a charming heaven nor a hideous hell. It is a mixture of both. Dhyana Yoga says that what the world is to us, depends upon ourselves. So long as we sell ourselves to the senses and subject ourselves to numerous passions, there is no hope of happiness for us in this world. But when we cease to send piteous petitions to the senses, when we have learnet to be our own masters, we find that misery never was. "For persons free from desire or hatred, for the persons who have controlled their mind, and who have realized the self, everywhere is found the bliss of Brahman [13](V-26)." Renunciation of sense pleasures therefore, should not be understood to mean asceticism and total abstinence from sense-pleasures; it is only keeping the senses under due control. Renunciation of the sense world – means that we should not allow ourselves too be enslaved by passionate sense - -desires, but should ever remain masters of those desires.

ध्यायतो वषियान्पुंसः सङ्गस्तेषूपजायतो
सङ्गात् संजायते कामः कामात्क्रोधोऽभजियायतो। II.62।।
क्रोधाद्भवति संमोहः संमोहात्स्मृतविभिर्रमः।
स्मृतभिर्रंशाद् बुद्धनिाशो बुद्धनिाशात्प्रणश्यतिा। II.63।।

"The person who constantly broods over objects of sense, gets attached to them, from attachment arises desires, and from desires, hatred; from hatred proceeds indiscrimination and from indiscrimination comes loss of the recollection of truth; from such loss of memory , the intellect is destroyed and one's ruin is thus complete."

"But enjoying the worldly things with senses free from desire or hatred and under due control, the self-controlled person attains calmness [14](II-64)." It is not sin to enjoy the sense-objects, and it is by no means advisable that all sense enjoyment is to be absolutely forsaken, for abandoning all sense-actions would be tantamount to reducing oneself to a clod of each or a block of stone. The only thing necessary is non-attachment and control of the senses. This is just the doctrine which the Upanishad preaches, when it says "तेन त्यक्तेन भुञ्जीथाः" "therefore enjoy with renunciation."

This gives the lie desire to the accusation sometimes brought against the Indian idea of renunciation, that it serves every tie, not only those of covetousness and evil passion but those likewise of duty and right affection. The Reverend N. Macnicol, for instance, holds this view of renunciation. He compares the method of renunciation with that of the religion of Christ and says "The goal of the one method of deliverance is Samadhi, Nirvana, Cessation of moral movement, silence attained by passing to great home of silence which is Brahman. The goal of the other is fulfillness of life and moral activity in unimpeded fellowship with the source of life-harmony, joy and peace in the perfect fulfillment of function, in the freedom and the blessedness of love gladly rendered to the Lord of Love."[15] Now, to show that the idea of Nirvana is fundamentally ill-conceived here, we have but to turn our attention to a single Sloka of the Gita: " It is they that reach the Nirvana of Brahman- those seers who are free from impurity, who have cut asunder their doubts, who are self-controlled and ever at work for the good of all beings [16](V-25)." The sloka speaks for itself. It says Nirvana is neither cessation of moral activity nor severance of the ties of affection, but the very opposite. Renunciation is not a severe frost killing the fair flower of right affection, but a warm sunshine to it. Renunciation does not sever brotherly ties but only nipe in the bud selfish ties. On the other hand, it opens the gates of the human heart as wide as not humanity above all but creation. Persons who have renounced selfishness are the only ones that can love God's children with any sincerity. The man of renunciation has indeed reached the home of solemn silence – the Brahman – he has indeed, attained the peace that passeth all understanding (शांति निर्वाणपरमाम, VI -15) – but his actions ever utter forth a glorious voice in reason's ears. Every single action of his preaches the glory of the Divine Essence in unmistakeable language to a sequacious[17] mind.

There is however a pseudo-renunciation which is justly to be condemned. It appears in many forms. In some it becomes laziness, and they assert that the giving up of activity is renunciation; in others, it takes the form of sense-hatred and they say that fleeing from the world to some secluded place is renunciation; in yet a third kind of people it assumes the form of ambition or greed and they want to give up their duty to try that of another, and to cover their mistake under the cloak of renunciation. Now, all such states of mind are the results of ignorance and not of enlightenment. On the other hand true renunciation proceeds from wisdom. It does not shun activity, much of less moral activity. It does not hate the world of senses, though it it does not hate the world of senses, though it does not lust after it. It does not give up duty, but feels unlimited joy, in discharging properly though disinterestedly whatever duites may devolve on it, on account of position in life.

Practice

So much for Vairagya or renunciation. We now turn to Abhayasa or practice. This practice is partly physical and partly mental. Physical practice will be the preliminary part, but the advanced and more important exercise will have to be mainly mental. Before beginning, the would be - Dhyana Yogin should first adjust his external life and regulate his food dress and habits. He will have to eat good food, wear plain dress and observe moderation in his habits. The Gita does not attach much importance to these questions, for minute rules in such particular are of no practical utility. It only states the principle: " For one who is moderate in eating and walking, who is moderate in his actions, and moderate in his sleep and wakefulness, Yoga becomes pleasant.[18](VI-7)." In brief, all extremes should be avoided; after first preparations one may begin practising.

He must select a clean sopt, say a room set apart for the purpose and there sitting in some convenient posture practice Yoga. First, he must learn to sit in a firm, erect posture. Then his eyes and other senses in their proper places so as not to allow them to wander away. This is all the physical portion of the practice. Now, the student may devote himself to the mind, (VI- 11, 12, 13).

Now comes the concentration of mind. This is the most difficult part. It cannot be achieved all at once. " Slowly and steadily, should one recede with a courageous mind; having made the mind to stand in Self, we should stop thinking of anything else. [19](VI-25)." The outgoing tendency of the mind is to be perseveringly checked. At first, it will be very difficult not to think of something outside, but as we go on separating ourselves, as it were, from the mind and what it is doing, the waves in the mental ocean begin gradually to subside. The mind when becomes an object of continued observation has the "trick" of becoming quite calm in time.

Spiritual Bliss

When calmness of mind is secured, we can realize ourselves as we are. Only then can we taste of real happiness, for all happiness is really inside, not outside. Just as in a flickering dim light a precious stone cannot be well examined and its worth correctly estimated, the true measure of happiness in a person cannot be seen by him of a wandering mind. But when he has attained tranquillity, he knows what happiness means. He then sees that absolute happiness is beyond the senses, to be enjoyed by a spiritual mind alone (VI-21). Even in the case of sense-pleasures, it is the mind that enables one to enjoy , for, if the mind be detached from the sense, the sense-perception will be of no avail. Now, there are several faculties in the mind, and these are at work in various fields busily digging out happiness. Thus one faculty gives us intellectual happiness while another confers upon us the moral pleasures. The pleasures of thought are finer than those of the senses and moral happiness is infinitely finer than both of them. But the faculty of self-concentration in its highly developed state gives us a feeling which is called not pleasure or happiness, but spiritual bliss. It is evident that no subtlety of thought could secure us the experience of such bliss. Just as the eye can only discern form but say nothing about sound, the intellectual faculty is no judge in matters of spiritual bliss. There is a special faculty in our mind which wishes to know what is bliss and this faculty works only when the mind has attained the power of self—concentration.

How do we know that this bliss is real and not an hallucination? Because once we begin to enjoy it, its destruction can never be conceived. When we do taste of it, our reason tells us that we always had this bliss in us and that we were never separated from it. If there were no such bliss already no exercise, spiritual or otherwise, could create it. This mine of felicity therefore is always within us. Happiness is ours by birth-right, but we have not had the good luck to use it. With infinite wealth hoarded at home we have gone out of ourselves to beg at the door of five poverty – striken senses.

When a man has realised true happiness or blessedness in himself, he sees happiness everywhere else, " To persons who have known the Self, the bliss of Brahman lies everywhere. (V- 26)[20]" As a person is so he sees the world. Our notions of the world are derived from our own mind. So this Yogin having realised happiness in himself, sees happiness in everyone else. In fact he sees the whole world to be one Boundless Ocean of Bliss, of which the individuals represent so many waves, great or small. Each one represents to him but the degree to which this Infinite Happiness has been manifested. Then it will be no mere intellectual assent with him to say that God indwells all beings, for, he never loses sight of God, being in eternal communion with Him, "He who sees Me everywhere and sees everything in Me, to him I do not become invisible nor is he away from Me. (VI- 30)[21]" Such a Yogi's attitude may be best described, thus: --

"Happiness is the only good.

The time to be happy is now,

The place to be happy is here.

The way to be happy is to make others so."

Secluded life and Service to Humanity

There is a consideration by the way. This Abhyasa or practice of Yoga necessarily implies frequent and sometimes prolonged retirement from not only bad society but also from good. First, it will be necessary to associate with good persons and to avoid the company of persons whose ideas disturb the mind. Then it will be found more convenient to be alone, to think and meditate alone. "The Yogin should always practice in privacy, alone and with the senses and mind controlled, with no desire or sense of possession. (VI -10)[22]" This recommendation of practice in solitude has led some to think that the Gita is self-contradictory in as much as it recommends service to humanity and retirement frm society at once. But this is an obvious misconception. The practice refers to a preparatory stage, while the service to a later. The Yogin practicing in seclusion can no more be blamed for his uselessness to the world than a student who goes for a time to the University to develop further his mental powers and to fit himself the better for life. The retirement of the Yogin will never take him to an utter blank wiped of all ideas of the universe, but it will bring him to this busy universe a richer and a wiser man offering the best fruits of his labours to all his brethren alike. The object of the Yogi's practice is not aimless thought, but a solemn preparation for useful life. All self-made men walked alone first and expected no others either to lead them or to accompany them in the noble and difficult path they chalked out for themselves. And then came the free mixing with society and ceaseless self-sacrifice. Ever in intimate touch with Reality (ब्रह्म संस्पर्श:) , they could help mankind to enjoy a similar bliss.

Indeed, it is the person who has by steady and preserving practice of devotion has realised the noble truth that the same Divine Essence lives in all beings, that can undertake with any sincerity and consciousness the taks of benefiting humanity. A dark ray of selflessness will have stolen into the heart of the noblest person who has not realised any such link connecting, as it were, all humanity into one living chain. The man of realisation, on the other hand, has reached a state in which he can have equal regard for all beings. He has attained to the highest state of "Evenness of mind." (VI-7-8).[23] In spite of heat of cold, pleasure or pain, praise or blame, the person who finding satisfaction in his knowledge and Anubhava (experience) remains immovable like the mountain and has conquered his senses is a Yogin that is perfect, to whom a lamp of earth, a block of stone, or a nugget of gold is the same. He has so far conquered his selfishness that nothing outside can influence him. And as for his behavior, it is the same to all; "He who has equal regard for benefactors, friends, foes, indifferent men, well-wishers, persons deserving of hatred, relatives, saints and sinners- he is the best Yogin (VI -9). [24]" how does the Yogin show equal regard for all these? By wishing and doing good to all alike. Whatever may be the action and attitude of the public towards him he himself remains the same. He always lives a live of sacrifice. He calls upon all alike to do good, not by precept but by example. He makes himself one with his brethren and his universal sympathy attracts all towards him. He feels compassion for all groaning under suffering, sorrow and sin. He feels with the righteous their delight and satisfaction in spiritual life. He is ever ready to minister to the sick, to instruct the ignorant, to help the weak, to guide the intelligent, and to lead spiritual aspirants to self—realisation. He, in fact, bridges the gulf between the man of the world and the Highest God. Such is the ideally perfect Yogin.

"But what if we are not perfect in this life? Are we not losers either way?" this is an objection raised by the philosophy of utility. "The sense enjoyment have been renounced by the Yogin and the higher bliss is not attained, what then/" Now, this objection assumes that sense enjoyments are sure and the Yogin has forsaken them, and further that spiritual bliss is not guaranteed and therefore not worth striving for. The hollowness of both these assumptions will be clear to any one who has seen from the preceding pages that the Yogin does not in reality renounce all sense enjoyment but only keeps the senses under control, and that the blissful nature of the human soul is undoubted fact, which has only to be discovered, as it were, to be enjoyed. But the Gita gives another reply to this question just to meet the objector on his own ground. "The man who has failed in Yoga is born in rich and noble families or still better he born in the family of wise Yogins themselves. A birth like this is indeed very difficult to attain. In that life, the man gets the same Yogic ideas that he had in his former body, and again strives for perfection. For, in spite of himself he is carried away by the instinctive past habit. Even an ordinary student, who studies Yoga experimentally gets beyond the ritualistic fruits, but the Yogin who exerts with energy becomes purified and attaining perfection after many births reaches the highest gal."

प्राप्य पुण्यकृतां लोकान्षत्विा शाश्वती: समा:।
शुचीनां श्रीमतां गेहे योगभ्रष्टोऽभजिायतो।।VI.41।।
अथवा योगनिामेव कुले भवतिधीमताम्।
एतद्धि दुर्लभतरं लोके जन्म यदीदृशम्।।VI.42।।
तत्र तं बुद्धसिंयोगं लभते पौर्वदेहिकम्।
यतते च ततो भूय: संसद्धिौ कुरुनन्दन।।VI.43।।
पूर्वाभ्यासेन तेनैव ह्रयिते ह्यवशोऽपि सि:।
जज्ञिासुरुपि योगस्य शब्दब्रह्मातविर्ततो।।VI.44।।

Reincarnation

The Gita does not attach much importance to the explanation of the much controverted question of Reincarnation but contents itself with giving some illustrations. It says that just as a person changes his old clothes for new ones, and just as the same man passes through different stages of life from childhood to old age, a person goes from body to body. We may conclude, therefore, that at the time of the Gita, as at present, the theory of re-incarnation was a settled doctrine with the Hindus[25] . Besides the Hindus, many other people have accepted the doctrine. In the scientific world, however, the belief in the doctrine is by no means universal. A great many scientists have written against it, while others equally illustrious have made assertions of their faith in the doctrine. Re-incarnation, on the whole, cannot be said to be a hopelessly absurd doctrine, for, after all that is said against it, thare are still many good features about it. We shall here give a few extracts from some of the most well-known writers of the West to show how these features are appreciated by them also: -

Prof. Max Muller says: "The popular mind of India seems never to have doubted the fact that every good or every evil thought or deed will grow and bear fruit, and that no one can ever escape from the consequences of his own acts and thoughts. Wheather such a belief is right or wrong is not the question, but it produced at all events a deep sense of responsibility. Instead of complaints about the injustice and cruelty of God, people were taught that what seemed underserved misfortunes, were fully deserved, were, in fact, the natural consequences of previous acts, and in one respect the safest means of paying off all debts. Philosophy at the same time held out a hope that in the end this net of consequences might be broken through, and the self, enlightened by true knowledge, might return to whence it came, return to himself and be himself; that is, be again the Universal Self, free for ever from the chains and pains of this transcient episode of life on earth."[26]

Prof. A. A. Macdonell remarks: "The immovable hold it acquired on Indian thought is doubtless due to the satisfactory explanation it offered of the misfortune or prosperity which is often clearly caused by no action done in this life. Indeed the Indian doctrine of transmigration, fantastic thought it may appear to us, has the two-fold merit of satisfying the requirements of justice in the moral government of the world, and at the same time in inculcating a valuable ethical principle which makes every man the architect of his own fate."[27]

Miss S. E. Waldo writes: " Reincarnation and Karma are inseparably connected together and these two great laws rightly and completely understood show man that he alone is the arbiter of his destiny, that he alone is the arbiter of his destiny, that he can no longer attribute his sorrows and sufferings to a mysterious Providence, that he can no longer trust to forms and creeds, but must arouse himself and set himself to correct past errors and learn to know his true nature."

It would not be difficult to cite many other similar questions. But it is only necessary here too point out that so far as the study of Dhyana Yoga is concerned, it is immaterial whether we accept the theory or not. Its practice and results concern the living present and not a doubtful future. Its one important purpose is to show men to keep up the balance of mind so as to be inured against outside influences. It does not entail belief in any theory whatever. The Yoga only proposes to point to a higher form of happiness than that obtained through the senses and says that happiness is subjective and not objective. To secure this or rather to realise the blissful nature which is the permanent privilege of the soul, the one means that Dhyana Yoga proposes is self—concentration aided by moral culture.

The Excellence of Dhyana Yoga

The Gita has warm commendations of this Yoga. "The Yogin is greater than the ascetic, he is held to be greater than even persons distinguished for intelligence, the Yogin is greater than the worker, therefore be thou a Yogin, Oh Arjuna (VI-46)."[28] We shall consider these statements in order. First the Yoga is better than asceticism. Asceticism in the sense of self –torture, is not only no passport to spirituality, but is also directly opposed to it. We have already quoted a sloka which recommends the avoidance of extremes in habits, as a qualification for the Yoga. Here is another Gita text which directly condemns it.

अशास्त्रविहितं घोरं तप्यन्ते ये तपो जनाः।

दम्भाहङ्कारसंयुक्ताः कामरागबलान्विताः॥ XVII.5॥

कर्षयन्तः शरीरस्थं भूतग्राममचेतसः।

मां चैवान्तःशरीरस्थं तान्विद्ध्यासुरनिश्चयान्॥ XVII.6॥

"Those men who practices unscriptural hard asceticism, coupled with hypocrisy and vanity, guided by lust of power and passion, know such people, to be of a demonical resolution, for they are tormenting the aggregate of beings, in the body, as also Me who am seated in the heart." Asceticism is comparatively easy of accomplishment. The most toilsome pilgrimages and the most painful penances are far easier and require infinitely less exertion than concentration of mind, and a moral life. It is only fair, however, to note here that all external religious practice does not deserve a wholesale condemnation. External forms, symbols, and practices are very often helps to quicken the birth of spiritual life; and it is for this reason that forms and ceremonies have found a place in many religions of the world. That the concrete suggests the abstract and helps quicker perception of the same is now almost a truism. The man who would have people take only the real spirit of religion and mercilessly reject all outward practices, is comparable to one who wishes that the cocoa palm should near fruit consisting of the kernel only, to the exclusion of the husk. The outward husk is not less useful merely because it is outside, for, it serves the important purpose of protecting the precious internal kernel. So, ascetic practices have worth of their own. But Yoga is their very kernel. Again, Yoga is higher than intellectual attainment. Reasons, no doubt, have its importance in the ascertainment of truth. But what is of much more importance to a man is that he actually realizes the truth he believes instead of being able to merely theories. Now, such an immediate perception is possible only to the Yogin or a person who has learnt to control and focus his mind on that which he wishes to ascertain. Merely reading books on religion, hearing intelligent lectures, and even reasoning on them, though in themselves valuable enough, will be of no avail, if we do not exercise the feelings in accordance with the conclusions of reasons. Lastly, Yoga is greater than Karma. If Karma is understood to mean ritual the sentence needs no further explanation, after what has been said above about Tapas. But if we interpret the word to mean work, a remark is necessary. All work is but the experience of thought, and the best deeds of the great man of the world represent but a fraction of their greatness represented by their thoughts. Mind-control is therefore vastly superior to works which are but the outward symbols of it. The world's greatest men are always calm, silent and unknown. Even when they do not work they are not lazy, for , their noble thoughts spread with infectious rapidity and influence thousands of good men who are thus stimulated to ceaseless activity. Thus the Dhyana Yogin is superior to the ascetic, superior to the philosopher and superior to the man of work. As Emerson says, "All men are commanded by the saint." He is the master of the universe. "Therefore become a Yogin." Exhorts Sri Krishna.

What is this Yoga?

योगस्थः कुरु कर्माणि सङ्गं त्यक्त्वा धनञ्जय।

सद्धिध्यसद्धिध्यो: समो भूत्वा समत्वं योग उच्यतो। II.48।।

"समत्वं योग उच्च्यते " or "Evenness of mind is Yoga." The Karma Yogin tries to control the thought-world by control of action, while the Dhyana Yogin controls his actions by thought control. Both are equally noble, for, thought and action are inseparably connected with each other. Really speaking therefore, nobody can be perfect Karma Yogin, unless he has learn the secret of control, and no one can get control over his mind, unless he has become a perfect Karma Yogin. Thought and action therefore have to be developed in parallel lines, the ideal of both being evenness or equanimity. This state is also called (समाधि) Samadhi which is a Sanskrit word meaning "adjustment of the mind". All ordinary men have experience of two states known as the conscious and the unconscious respectively, the conscious being a higher state than the unconscious. In this unconscious state the functions of the mind are as it were dormant, stupefied or stunted, and in the conscious state they are all working. By experiences of deep contemplation and devotion, the Yogin claims that the mind can be developed into a still higher state, where the mental faculties reach such a fineness, that the mind knows without reasoning, feels without passion and wills without egoism. This state is Samadhi and he whose self-control has resulted in this supreme state of mind is called SAMAHITA (well-poised), YUKTA (attuned to Yoga) and a PARAMAYOGIN (the best of Yogins).

[1] From a consideration of Slokas 10 to 17 of Chapter VI, which is expressly named Dhyana Yoga, it will be clear that this Yoga might be called "ASHTANGA YOGA" as generally known. But we have preserved the name "Dhyana Yoga" not only because the other word is nowhere used in the Gita, but also because of the eight steps to Yoga(Raja Yoga) the first five are considered the external in contradiction to those beginning with Dhyana which are internal (or primary).

[2] ये हि संस्पर्शजा भोगा दुःखयोनय एव ते ।
आद्यन्तवन्तः कौन्तेय न तेषु रमते बुधः ॥5.22॥

[3] "बाह्यस्पर्शेष्वसक्तात्मा विन्दत्यात्मनि यत्सुखम् ।
स ब्रह्मयोगयुक्तात्मा सुखमक्षयमश्नुते ॥V.21॥

[4] इन्द्रियाणां हि चरतां यन्मनोऽनुविधीयते ।
तदस्य हरति प्रज्ञां वायुर्नावमिवाम्भसि ॥II.67॥

[5] चञ्चलं हि मनः कृष्ण प्रमाथि बलवद्दृढम् ।
तस्याहं निग्रहं मन्ये वायोरिव सुदुष्करम् ॥VI-34॥

[6] आरुरुक्षोर्मुनेर्योगं कर्म कारणमुच्यते योगारूढस्य तस्यैव शमः कारणमुच्यते ॥VI-3 ॥;

[7]In tis verse the word Karma is restricted to rutuals by some. Even then the Sloka should be understood to mean that rites and rituals are intended as a preliminary step to rouse soul, but real religion begins only with feeling of spiritual calmness. This is in effect the same as saying that Tamas is to be renounced before Rajas.

[8] कर्मेन्द्रियाणि संयम्य य आस्ते मनसा स्मरन् । इन्द्रियार्थान्विमूढात्मा मिथ्याचारः स उच्यते ॥III -6॥

यस्त्विन्द्रियाणि मनसा नियम्यारभतेऽर्जुन । कर्मेन्द्रियैः कर्मयोगमसक्तः स विशिष्यते ॥III.7॥

[9] यदा हि नेन्द्रियार्थेषु न कर्मस्वनुषज्जते ।
सर्वसङ्कल्पसंन्यासी योगारूढस्तदोच्यते ॥VI.4॥

[10] उद्धरेदात्मनाऽऽत्मानं नात्मानमवसादयेत् ।
आत्मैव ह्यात्मनो बन्धुरात्मैव रिपुरात्मनः ॥VI.5॥

[11] यं लब्ध्वा चापरं लाभं मन्यते नाधिकं ततः ।
यस्मिन्स्थितो न दुःखेन गुरुणापि विचाल्यते ॥VI-22॥

[12] योऽयं योगस्त्वया प्रोक्तः साम्येन मधुसूदन।
एतस्याहं न पश्यामि चञ्चलत्वात् स्थिति स्थिराम्।।VI.33।।

[13] "कामक्रोधवियुक्तानां यतीनां यतचेतसाम्।
अभितो ब्रह्मनिर्वाणं वर्तते विदितात्मनाम्।।V.26।।"

[14] रागद्वेषवियुक्तैस्तु विषयानिन्द्रियैश्चरन्।
आत्मवश्यैर्विधेयात्मा प्रसादमधिगच्छति।।II.64।।

[15] *The Religion of Jesus, by the Reverend Macnicol, M.A.*

[16] लभन्ते ब्रह्मनिर्वाणमृषयः क्षीणकल्मषाः।
छिन्नद्वैधा यतात्मानः सर्वभूतहिते रताः।।V.25।।

[17] *Meaning: (of a person) lacking independence or originality of thought.*

[18] यतात्मनः प्रशान्तस्य परमात्मा समाहितः।
शीतोष्णसुखदुःखेषु तथा मानापमानयोः।।VI.7।।

[19] शनैः शनैरुपरमेद् बुद्ध्या धृतिगृहीतया।
आत्मसंस्थं मनः कृत्वा न किञ्चिदपि चिन्तयेत्।।VI.25।।

[20] कामक्रोधवियुक्तानां यतीनां यतचेतसाम्।
अभितो ब्रह्मनिर्वाणं वर्तते विदितात्मनाम्।।V.26।।

[21] यो मां पश्यति सर्वत्र सर्वं च मयि पश्यति।
तस्याहं न प्रणश्यामि स च मे न प्रणश्यति।।VI.30।।

[22] योगी युञ्जीत सततमात्मानं रहसि स्थितः।
एकाकी यतचित्तात्मा निराशीरपरिग्रहः।।VI.10।।

[23] यतात्मनः प्रशान्तस्य परमात्मा समाहितः।
शीतोष्णसुखदुःखेषु तथा मानापमानयोः।।VI.7।।

ज्ञानविज्ञानतृप्तात्मा कूटस्थो विजितेन्द्रियः।
युक्त इत्युच्यते योगी समलोष्टाश्मकाञ्चनः।।VI.8।।

[24] "सुहृन्मित्रार्युदासीनमध्यस्थद्वेष्यबन्धुषु।
साधुष्वपि च पापेषु समबुद्धिर्विशिष्यते।। VI -9।।

[25] *"The theory that every individual passes after death into a series of new existences in heaven or hell or in the bodies of men and animals or in labts on earth where it is rewarded or punished for all deeds in the 6ᵗʰ Century B.C., that Buddha received it without questions." – (Page 386, History of Sanskrit Literature, by Prof. A.A. Macdonell.)*

[26] *Six Systems of Indian Philosophy (Page 511)*

[27] *History of Sanskrit Literature , page 388.*

[28] तपस्विभ्योऽधिको योगी ज्ञानिभ्योऽपि मतोऽधिकः।
कर्मिभ्यश्चाधिको योगी तस्माद्योगी भवार्जुन।।VI.46।।

CHAPTER THREE

Jnana Yoga

Jnana (knowledge) in the Vedanta philosophy plays a part which neither work nor love nor yet meditation does. The Upanishads are never tired of praising knowledge, and they make it the *sine qua non* of salvation. The Bhagavadgita as the best symposium of all genuine Upanishadic doctrines is no less warm in its encomiums on Jnana.

"Even if thou be the most sinful of all sinners all sin thou shalt cross over with the aid of the boat of knowledge alone."

अपि चेदसि पापेभ्य: सर्वेभ्य: पापकृत्तम:।

सर्वं ज्ञानप्लवेनैव वृजिनं सन्तरिष्यसि॥4.36॥

"Knowing which you will be free from all evils." "Knowing, with which all sages attained supreme perfection."

परं भूय: प्रवक्ष्यामि ज्ञानानां ज्ञानमुत्तमम्।

यज्ज्ञात्वा मुनय: सर्वे परां सिद्धिमितो गता:॥ XIV.1 ॥

"Knowing which one reaches immortality." These slokas bear testimony to the very high place which the author of the Gita accords to Jnana.

Knowledge is not mere Speculation

But what is this Jnana? Some have thought that it is no more than a speculative process and the relation that man enters into with God or the Highest Truth whatever that may be, is often erroneously identified with vain enjoyments and conjectures of reason to the exclusion of all moral sympathy and affection. That the exposition of the philosophy of Janana Yoga necessarily requires the exercise of reason just as much as other Yogas do or even a little more, is admitted. It is to the credit of this Yoga that it uses the best instrument yet known to man for the ascertainment of the truth. The dizzy height to which reason ascends in this Yoga does, it is conceded, prove too much for undeveloped intellects. But to say that it ignores morality or is opposed to it, is, to be mild, an untruth. Philosophy opposed to religion and morality is unknown to Vedantic works in general and to the Gita in particular. The Jnana of the Gita is not merely reasoned belief, though this knowledge is by no means against the use of the intellectual faculty. This Jnana is nothing short of the realisation of the one truth worthy of knowing, and living up to the conclusion of practical reason.

Qualification for Jnana

Knowledge as properly understood is the accumulation of information – a collection of all past experience of men. But real knowledge is a reference to ourselves. Original knowledge is possible only when we turn away from books, teachers and instructors and literally educate ourselves (draw forth our wisdom). All great men whether of religion, philosophy or science, discovered knowledge not in books or other outside help but in themselves. Of course the vat store of knowledge handed down by our forefathers deserves respect and worth careful study. Certainly guides and teachers are necessary to suggest methods. The Gita in full recognition of this says:

तद्वद्धि प्रणिपातेन परिप्रश्नेन सेवया।

उपदेक्ष्यन्ति ते ज्ञानं ज्ञानिनस्तत्त्वदर्शिनः॥ IV.34॥

"Know that this knowledge is got by reverence, enquiry, with humility and personal service rendered unto teachers. These knowers who have seen the truth will initiate you into knowledge. (IV- 34)." But unless the aspirant exerts himself with the necessary qualifications, nothing results from mere outside help. A teacher can suggest methods and remove obstructions, and there his business ends. If you wish that I should share with you the enjoyment of a beautiful picture, all that you can do, is to show me that picture, and to command it to me. But if I have not the eye for beauty, can you help? And if I happen to be short—sighted, how could you help? You may give me a pair of glasses, and thus assist me a little, that is all. But the innate defect cannot be cured. So unless there are the requisite qualifications, the student is not fit for Jnana Yoga. These qualifications are enumerated in the following sloka:

श्रद्धावाँल्लभते ज्ञानं तत्परः संयतेन्द्रियः।

ज्ञानं लब्ध्वा परां शान्तिमचिरेणाधिगच्छति॥IV.39॥

" The man of faith who is preserving and has controlled the senses attains knowledge. (IV – 39) ." To a person working with these requisites, knowledge unfailingly shines forth of itself.

Let us now examine these three pre-requisites. In the first place, faith is necessary. Nothing was ever achieved without faith. In Carlyle's words, "Faith is great, life giving." Religion without faith, philosophy without faith, is dry as dust. Faith is not blind belief or a mere mental assent to a doctrine. It is an innate faculty of man, through which we work out and find the truth. When looking at a certain obvious set of phenomena in external nature or in the mind, we leap to the conclusion that there must be a more complicated set behind them, we exercise faith. To find out the purpose of a new machine, which we never saw before, we exercise our faith and find it out. Finding out the true significance of letters and words of a forgotten ancient language requires the exercise of faith. This faith is quite necessary for the student of Jnana Yoga. The person who studies nature as a whole and sees in it an infinite series of shifting scenes is forced to ask himself, "Is this real? If not, what is real?" His heart becomes possessed of the one strong belief that there must be something permanent behind this constantly changing nature and he strives accordingly to find it out. First, he has the faith in himself. He is fully convinced that he has the instrument and capacity required for the search. Secondly he is as fully persuaded that there is a Reality in this changing Universe and is worth knowing, a reality in fact,

यो यो यां यां तनुंभक्तः श्रद्धयार्चतिमिच्छति।

तस्य तस्याचलां श्रद्धां तामेव वदिधाम्यहम्।। VII.21।।

"Knowing which nothing remains to be known. (VII-2)"

It is this intense faith that saves a man. "The person who without knowledge and without faith indulges in doubt, destroys himself; for the sceptic there is neither this world nor the other, nor is there happiness for him. (IV- 40)" there is of course a wise harmless skepticism which is quite necessary for everyone. We should all weigh well, and consider well before we believe. But the sceptic[1] whose creed is made of denial and doubt, a person whose motto is universal unbelief is dangerous to himself as well as to society. No happiness material or spiritual can exist for him. For all progress, at least a tentative faith is necessary, and there is no where else so much need for this as in religion. This faith as distinguished from assumption and superstitious belief is the first qualification for Jnana Yoga.

In the second place, persistence is required for such a student. Enlightenment does not come in a moment. First, the truth has to be heard. Reading of good books and listening to expositions of wise men is the very first step. Many have neither the inclination nor the capacity for enjoying abstract thoughts. Well has the Kathopanishad declared that ,"Many cannot hope even to hear of God." "श्रवणायापि बहुभिर्यो न लभ्य्य: " This hearing proposes a dissatisfaction with the existing state of things and an intense desire to find something more trustworthy. The ordinary man knows that the world is an awful mixture of good and evil and snatches what pleasures he can. He wants to make the best of it. He receives harder and harder blows but does not awaken. When after hard experience, he learns that it is difficult to enjoy without suffering, and that he must go beyond the world of sense enjoyment to get the infinite peace of mind, he exercises his faith. His heart then tells him that behind the pairs of opposite, there is something very permanent. It is then he begins to hear about God and other things of the sort. This hearing is the first step. The second step is to think over what has been heard. Mere hearing would be no avail if we never bestowed any after-thought on the matter. We should think it out day and night, till it becomes a habit with us. As a philosopher says, "आसपूतरेामतृ कालन्नयदेवदान्तचन्तिया" " The whole time up to sleep, the whole period of life up to death if necessary, is to be spent in thinking on truth." This thinking occupies a most important part in Jnana Yoga. Reason is to be pushed to its utmost limit and legitimate conclusion here. No church or creed, no book or doctrine, no authority of how-so-ever reputed an infalliability, should be deemed sufficient to form a belief unless reason is satisfied in the matter. To follow right reason where so-ever it may lead us, and cheerfully to take the consequences with undaunted courage, must be spirit with which the student of Jnana Yoga works. After this thinking comes the profound meditation of the truths so thought out. Reasoning by itself is not sufficient. It can wipe off superstitions and it can dispel doubts. The truth, to which reason points, should be meditated upon, felt and should also be made the very essence of practical life. When we are convinced of what is the truth, our business must be to live the truth. To feel truth intensely till we are identified with it as it were, is the third and last step. It is then that realisation is complete and one becomes a Jnana Yogin. To be willing to have this dogged persistence throughout, to patiently hear, think, and to feel till we realise the truth is the second qualification required of the student of Jnana Yoga.

Finally, the control of the senses, is an absolutely necessary qualification of the would-be Jnana Yogin. For, many temptations come in his way. The first temptation will be to think that it is foolish to try transcend the senses. The sense-pleasures are so dazzling that they sometimes induce us to think with the Old Charvakas (Materialists of ancient India) that all religion and philosophy is the concoction of fools or cheats. To think that life is well enough and that we need not bother ourselves at all about anything beyond, will be the first temptation. Again, love of sensuality may tempt us to imagine an eternal future world or a future state in which we shall have all play and no work, all good and no evil, where we shall eat, drink and make merry but never suffer. But the student of Jnana Yoga has to see clearly satisfied as to the hollowness and destructible nature of all sensual pleasure either here or hereafter. We may accumulate as much as we like of the means to sense—enjoyment, we may get the patronage of Kings or even Gods to assist us in such accumulation, but at the end of such enjoyment we are certain to be miserable. " Having enjoyed the vast world of pleasure, they then at the end of their good fortune enter the world of mortals.

अमी हि त्वां सुरसङ्घाः वशिनृति
कंचेदिभीताः पुराञ्जलयो गृणन्ति
सुवस्तीत्युक्त्वा महर्षसिद्धिसङ्घाः
स्तुवन्ति त्वां स्तुतिभिः पुष्कलाभिः॥IX.21॥

"Sense—indulgence ends in death and destruction, but control of the senses leads Godward; knowing this one should constantly exercise sense-control. This is the third qualification for Jnana Yoga. (IX – 21)."

The Knowledge in Jnana Yoga

The Knowledge of Kshetra and Kshetrajna spoken
of as "The Knowledge" in
Jnana Yoga

Which is the knowledge to be gained by such a student? It is the knowledge of matter and soul and their distinguishing properties. What knowledge is more important than that which concerns our ownselves, and our relations to our surroundings? That part of philosophy that deals with the essence of ultimate truths, the reality in us as well as in other things around us, is justly regarded as the Crown of philosophy. Sri Krishna accordingly says :

क्षेत्रज्ञं चापि मां विद्धि सर्वक्षेत्रेषु भारत।

क्षेत्रक्षेत्रज्ञयोर्ज्ञानं यत्तज्ज्ञानं मतं मम।। XIII.3।।

" The knowledge of Kshetra and Kshetrajna is that which is deemed by Me as the best knowledge. (XIII -3).

Now, Kshetrajna and Kshetra are in modern philosophy known as subject and object respectively, and we may use these terms in connection with the Gita also if we keep in mind the following description: -

We shall first consider the teaching of the Gita about the Kshetra (the object)

महाभूतान्यहङ्कारो बुद्धिरव्यक्तमेव च।

इन्द्रियाणि दशैकं च पञ्च चेन्द्रियगोचराः।। XIII.6।।

" The great elements, Ahankara, Buddhi and Avyakta, the ten senses and the one mind and the five objects of the sense; desire and hatred, pleasure and pain, the aggregate, intelligence, firmness – this here describes in brief, is the Kshetra with its modifications (XIII 6—7)."

To put this in more intelligible or rather modern language – the senses together with their objects (whether forming our own bodies i.e. objects outside) which constitute gross matter, and the mind with all its modifications, known to eastern philosophy as subtle matter, are the Kshetra (object). That the gross body and the gross things around us are objects of knowledge and as such depend on a subject is almost self-evident to any one. But that the mind is no less an object – though finer and subtler than other objects – is a little difficult to understand. But this will be clear on a little reflection. Desiring or hating, feeling happy or miserable and performing other similar functions, the mind is itself subject to constant fluctuations; for , it grows, develops and decays. These changes of the mind no less than those of the body, are the object of the knowledge of a something which must be itself changeless. The changes of the mind and the changes of the body act and react on each other, but stand ever separate from their cogniser. All these changes, gross and subtle, of the body as well as of the mind, form the Kshetra.

Let us now turn to Kshetrajna. "He who knows this Kshetra is called Kshetrajna by the knowers of these (the subject and the object)." The body has no intelligence of its own, it cannot be self –conscious. Nor can the mind, if we take mind to mean that which desires, hates, wills, imagines, remembers, doubts, reflects, thinks and performs various other functions.

But that which subsists all the changes of the mind, and recognises all such changes as a witness unaffected by them, must be itself changeless and this enduring aspect of ourselves is what is known as Atman and Kshetrajna.

Subject and Object presupposed in every Knowledge

Before entering into a detailed examination of Kshetrajna, it will be necessary to consider one important point. All knowledge presupposes subject and object or Kshetra and Kshetrajna as Gita calls them. We cannot therefore conceive of the beginning or cause of either the subject or the object, for even that conception should have to presuppose subject and object. Hence the Gita says,

प्रकृतिं पुरुषं चैव विद्ध्यनादी उभावपि।

विकारांश्च गुणांश्चैव विद्धि प्रकृतिसंभवान्।। XIII.20।।

"Know that Prakriti and Purusha are both beginningless (XIII-20)."

This Prakriti is the same as Kshetra , for, the next half of the same Sloka says "Know that the modifications and Gunas (Satwam, Rajas and Tamas) are born of Prakriti." We have already referred to the Gunas while discussion Karma Yoga. All the changes brought about by the forces of nature whether these changes be gross or subtle are in Prakriti or Kshetra. Kshetrajna is also known as Purusha or Person. The Gita thus defines the Prakriti and Purusha:

कार्यकारणकर्तृत्वे हेतुः प्रकृतिरुच्यते।

पुरुषः सुखदुःखानां भोक्तृत्वे हेतुरुच्यते।। XIII.21।।

" That which is the one occasion of cause and effect and agony, is called Prakriti; the perceiver of pleasure and pain, is said to be Purusha. (XIII – 21) " Here we must notice that casualty is possible only in time and space. Therefore that which philosophers call "देशकाल निमित्त .."[2] or space, time and casuality is included in Prakriti. That which, so to speak, senses or feelings, is the Purusha. All human knowledge is based upon this distinction and opposition of Purusha and Prakriti, of Kshetra and Kshetrajna or as we may now express it, of subject and object.

यावत्संजायते किञ्चित्सत्त्वं स्थावरजङ्गमम्।

क्षेत्रक्षेत्रज्ञसंयोगात्तद्विद्धि भरतर्षभ।। XIII.27।।

"Whatever is born, whether unmoving or moving , know that to be from a commingling of Kshetra and Ksetrajna, Oh, the best of Bharata's race! (XIII—27)"

The natural purity of the Soul

We have already seen that the essence of Kshetra is to be changing. We have also seen that Kshetrajna to be the perceiver of this change must itself be changeless. But it is with our experience that Kshetrajna or Purusha has also the knack of identifying itself with pleasure, pain or with someone having modification of the mind. This double aspect of Kshetrajna, it is important to remember, for, from this circumstance, Jnana Yoga deduces a valuable corollary. According to Janna Yoga, the soul is by nature pure and happy, but gets into sorrow and suffering by its identification with Prakriti or change.

पुरुष: प्रकृतिस्थो हि भुङ्क्ते प्रकृतिजान्गुणान्।

कारणं गुणसङ्गोऽस्य सदसद्योनिजन्मसु॥XIII.22॥

" The Purusha experiences the Gunas of nature by identification with Prakriti; the cause of such experience (of soul) in good or bad life, is its attachment to the Gunas. (XIII -22)." This self-identification with Prakriti is Ajnana (ignorance) and pleasure and pain is SAMSARA (circling round) as popularly called by Vedantic philosophers.

Ignorance

Jnana Yoga therefore preaches that the self is always free, and bondage is nothing but this ignorance or identification with Prakriti.

नादत्ते कस्यचित्पापं न चैव सुकृतं विभुः।

अज्ञानेनावृतं ज्ञानं तेन मुह्यन्ति जन्तवः॥V.15॥

"Knowledge is enveloped in ignorance, it is hence that beings befool themselves. (V- 15)." This is the most logical position about the self or soul, for the soul cannot be both free and bound at the same time. If it is bound, that is , if its nature is to sow and reap sweet and bitter fruits, if this be its essential nature then nothing can make it free. For, as the great Sureswaracharya says,

Description: I:\Geetai-Mission-2022\The Heart of The Bhagavadgita\Picture1.jpg

"If the Atman is of the nature of a doer, etc., then do not hope for freedom therefrom; for the nature of things cannot be removed just as for instance, the heat of the sun (cannot be removed)." If it is our nature to be subject to fluctuations of pleasure and pain, what is the good of trying to alter it? If on the other hand, the self is pure and free, by nature, it is impossible for anything outside to influence it or make it bound. Hence the ancient philosophers of India contended that the soul is by nature free, and that the only real bondage is ignorance. पूरकारान्तरा संभावादवविके एव बन्ध: " As there can be no alternative, (we have to admit that) indiscrimination is the only bondage, " says the Sankhya Sutra (VI -16).

Description: I:\Geetai-Mission-2022\The Heart of The Bhagavadgita\Picture2.jpg

Ignorance is the productive filed of the following (four pain- bearing obstructions) whether these be dormant, attenuated, overpowered or expanded," says the Yoga Sutra (II – 4)

Description: I:\Geetai-Mission-2022\The Heart of The Bhagavadgita\Picture3.jpg

"duḥkha-janma-pravṛttidoṣa-mithyājñānānām uttarottarāpāye tadanantarā pāyāt apavargaḥ (1.1.2:)"

"Misery, birth, activity (with attachments), sin, false knowledge, of these those following in succession being removed, the immediately preceding in each case is removed and the result is freedom," says Nyaya Sutra (I -1.2).

Hence it follows that the experience of the pleasure and pains of this world is only while ignorance lasts. It is only apparent, but the real nature of the soul is freedom. All great men have preached this idea and all religions preach that the apparent life of man is an empty dream,[3] and weakness is not the essential nature of the soul. The individual soul was originally pure and perfect, and this purity and perfection is to be regained once more. This is a universal idea. The Mahabharata says that at first, all men were righteous. And then error began to assail their hearts. This clouded their perception and they became covetous. Covetousness gave rise to further confusion and then the Vedas disappeared. The story of Adam's fall by Satan's influence has a similar meaning behind it. According to Zoroastrianism, man's deterioration is due to Ahriman's influence. The Buddhistic theory of NIRVANA also implies this doctrine. All religious accounts of man's downfall agree in this, that the downfall has been due to man's own folly. This fault no other than ignorance; For, how else could a pure soul degrade itself? Therefore only the wise man who has attained knowledge realises this freedom.

ज्ञानेन तु तदज्ञानं येषां नाशतिमात्मन:।

तेषामादित्यवज्ज्ञानं प्रकाशयति तत्परम्।। V.16।।

"To those however, whose ignorance has been dispelled by enlightenment, knowledge like the bright sun reveals the Highest. (V- 16)."

It is only a wise man that knows that Kshetrajna is eternally free, changeless, and as such the only reality.

The Gita on the Real

We have stated at the commencement of this book that the Bhagavadgita is Brahma-Vidya, the philosophy of the Real and Yoga-Sastra, the science of Yoga or Equanimity.[4] This is a fit occasion to consider what the Gita has to say on the question of the Real since in Jnana Yoga the knowledge of Brahman or the Real and the means to the realization there of over each other. The Gita says,

नासतो विद्यते भावो नाभावो विद्यते सतः।

उभयोरपि दृष्टोऽन्तस्त्वनयोस्तत्त्वदर्शभिः।।II.16।।

"Of the unreal there is no existence, and of the Real there is no no-existence, - the true nature of both (the Real and the Unreal) has been found out by seers of truth (II -16)."

According to this definition, therefore, that which ceases to be at any time cannot claim to be regarded as Real. Applying this definition, we find that no one thing in the world satisfies this test except Universal consciousness or as the Gita with the Upanishads calls it the Brahman.

About Brahman, the teachings of the Gita present the condensed essence of all the Upanishads. In fact, the word Brahman, denoting the ultimate reality, and the various epithets applied to Brahman in Gita are all directly from the Uapnishads themselves. As if to confirm this view, the author calls his book itself an Upanishad, though according to tradition the Gita has been generally regarded as a Smriti in contradiction to Sruti under which head the Upanishads are always classed. The full title of the work "Bhagavadgitopanishad" as has been already pointed out and this clearly shows that the authir intended the work to be an essence of the Upanishads. The view is endorsed by the verse

"सर्वोपनिषिदो गावो , दोग्धा गोपाल नन्दनः।

पार्थो वत्सः सुधीर्भोक्ता , दुग्धं गीतामृतं महत् ।। (गीता महात्म्यम)

"All the Upanishads are kine,[5] Krishna is the milkman, Arjuna is the calf, and wise men the enjoyers of the ambrosia Gita, which is thus milked."

Now, the ventral doctrine of the Upanishads is that while the objective world is ever changing, the subject, the soul, never changes and is therefore the only reality The Gita refers to this important Upanishadic doctrine, when it says " Of the real there is no non-existence." According to Jnana Yoga, then, this reality being our own self there is no fear of its ever dying. For, reality is that which never changes or dies. That which witnesses all changes must be itself changeless, and therefore, says the Gita, for the person who has realised his true self there can be no more misery, fear or any other imperfection. The Kshetrajna is, in fact, perfect; but through ignorance he is thought imperfect. He is the changeless Reality, but trembles in fear of misery and death. To put it in Emerson's language "Every man is God playing the fool."

A thick veil of ignorance envelops us. Error has assailed us according to the Mahabharata. The sin of Adam has descended unto us according to the Christians. The temptations of Mara have enticed us according to the Buddhists. It is the same fact, put in different language. "अज्ञानेनावृतम ज्ञानम" " Knowledge is enveloped in ignorance." We have to overcome this ignorance, we have to take off this veil for then there will be no more fear, no more misery, no more death. The person who has realised the real self sees that misery never was, but all misery came through identification with Prakriti and her acts.

य एन वेत्ति हन्तार यश्चैन मन्यत हतम्।

उभौ तौ न वजिानीतो नाय हन्ति नि हन्यतो।। II.19।।

" He who considers him to be the killer, and he who thinks killed, both of these know not; for he neither killer nor is killed (II – 19)."

न जायत म्रयित वा कदाचि न्नाय भूतूवा भवति वा न भूयः।

अजो नित्यः शाश्वतोऽय पुराणो न हन्यत हन्यमान शरीरो।। II.20।।

" He is neither born nor does he ever die; nor will he having existed cease to exist again; unborn, ever-lasting, unchangeable, and primeval, he is never killed when the body is killed (II -20)."

Jnani's actlessness – What it means.

This view of the purity and actlessness of the soul has sometimes evoked undesereved criticism. Bishop Caldwell for instance, thus remarks on the Gita doctrine – " A man accused of murder neither denies his guilt nor pleads that he committed the act in self defence but addresses the Court in the language of Krishna. It is needless," he says, "to trouble yourselves about the enquiry any further , for it is impossible that any murder can have taken place. The soul can neither kill, nor be killed. It is either eternal or indestructible. Death is inevitable, and another birth is equally inevitable. It is not the part, therefore, of wise men like Judges of this Court to trouble themselves about such things." Would the Judge regard this defence as conclusive? Certainly not. Nor would it be regarded as a conclusive defence by the friends of the murdered person or by the world at large? The criminal might borrow from the Gita as many sound nothings as he liked, but the moral sense of the community would continue to regard his murder as a crime." Now, the Judge of the Court if they had any humour at all to pay this supposed murderer in the same coin, could easily give him the following reply: " Please note that the soul neither enquires nor sentences you to punishment. Besides, no harm can be done to your soul by punishment, for really it is beyond all punishment, being eternal and indestructible. But your body and mind disregarded the purity of the soul, and paid no respect to the pure soul enshrined in the body; so they will have to be punished." The impure mind of a murderer can have no conception of the purity of the soul. There is no reason whatever, therefore, to suppose that the ideas of freedom and purity of the soul preached to the world would produce any difficulty in practical life. On the other hand , there is every hope that it will prove a sure foundation for moral life. If one is made to believe that he is pure and free by nature and that this purity has to be manifested, he would know that to commit anything wrong is self—degradation while to do anything right is a step towards the re-attainment of self—purity. Hence any fear that this doctrine might prove dangerous to practical life should be considered entirely groundless.

"But," it may be asked, "what about the doctrine of the soul's being inactive, - the theory that it never acts nor is acted upon? Does it not lead men to laziness and indifference?" this objection owefully misunderstands the teachings. The soul is according to Jnana Yoga certainly beyond work, that is, work can produce no effect on it. In this sense the soul is no doubt actless.

"अनादत्विान्नरि्गुणत्वात्परमात्मायमव्ययः।

शरीरस्थोऽपि कौन्तेय न करोतनि लपि्यतो।।XIII.32।। "

" This understanding of supreme soul, being beginningless and void of Gunas, though seated in body, Oh , son of Kunti, neither acts nor is defiled (by acts)." But this does not mean that the soul identifies itself with Tamas and becomes inactive. Inactivity or indifference is the lowest manifestation of Prakriti, whereas the real soul is not only above Tamas and Rajas but also above Satwam. Hence its nearest approach is Satwic action is in reality actlessness. The Jnana Yoga, indeed, is compelled by no necessity to work, for he has realised his pure nature which is beyond work or duty.

यस्त्वात्मरतिरेव स्यादात्मतृप्तश्च मानवः।
आत्मन्येव च सन्तुष्टस्तस्य कार्यं न विद्यते।।III.17।।
नैव तस्य कृतेनार्थो नाकृतेनेह कश्चन।
न चास्य सर्वभूतेषु कश्चिदर्थव्यपाश्रयः।।III.18।।

" He who rejoices in the self and is satisfied in the self only, for him there is nothing to do; for him there is no interest either in what is done or what is not done here, nor is there in all beings anything on which he has to depend." He is beyond all selflessness and selfless work is therefore impossible for him. But for this reason it cannot be argued that Jnanin is precluded from doing any action. He works for the well – being of the world not by any selfish desire or by a sense of duty, but because it has become his habit to work selflessly.

सक्ताः कर्मण्यविद्वांसो यथा कुर्वन्ति भारत।
कुर्याद्विद्वांस्तथासक्तश्चिकीर्षुर्लोकसंग्रहम्।। III.25।।

" A wise man desirous of effecting Loka Sangraha without attachment should also work, Oh, descendant of Bharata, just as the ignorant do with attachment to action" (III – 25) ." Loka Sangraha is harmony or welding hearts together. This working for harmony is the very characteristic of the ideal Jnana Yogin, for it is only in such work that the actless Brahman is realised. Hence it is stated elsewhere,

"कर्म खल्वपि हि कर्तव्यं जातेनामतिरकर्शन ।
अकर्माणो हि जीवन्ति स्थावरा नेतरे जनाः ।।"

" A wise one should work here, Oh, tormentor of foes; those that are inactive are the inanimate things but not human beings." Therefore when a Jnani is said to be actless, it should never be understood that he leads a lazy life. Every man works for himself. But the idea of ordinary men about the life is very narrow. The Jnani also works for the self, but the self in his case is identified with the Real Self of the entire universe. Hence his work is for Loka-Sangraha[6] which literally means "embracing the whole world". He never works for a single body, he works for all bodies. He never works for a single mind, he works for all minds. His activity is therefore the most intense. Only he has realised that all selfish action is foolish and also that the Real Self being beyond Prakriti (time, space and causation) is in reality beyond action.

The nature of KSHETRAJNA

But to pursue our enquiry into the nature of Kshetrajna, We have seen that Kshetrajna is really pure and perfect, being ever beyond all limitations, time, space and casuality.[7] Having no limitations therefore Kshetrajna must be really infinite, and as we cannot conceive of two infinites, it follows that the reality behind all phenomena is one and the same. This is what Sri Krishna declares :

क्षेत्रज्ञं चापि मां विद्धि सर्वक्षेत्रेषु भारत।

क्षेत्रक्षेत्रज्ञयोर्ज्ञानं यत्तज्ज्ञानं मतं मम।।XIII.3।।

" Know Kshetrajna to be Me, In all Kshetras, Oh, descendant of Bharata. (XIII -3)" Thus Kshetrajna is in reality no other than Brahman. Now, another fact remains to be considered. This unchanging universal consciousness or Brahman, which is the self of things is the only Reality, for it satisfies the definition "Of the real there is no non-existence." It never ceases to exist. The objective things not satisfying this test of reality are therefore unreal. The objects being unreal, the subjectivity of Kshetrajna is also seen to be unreal; for the subject is inconceivable without an object. From the highest standpoint of philosophy, therefore, the Brahman or supreme self is neither subject nor object though it is the reality behind both. Hence the Gita calls both Kshetra and Kshetrajna, manifestations of the supreme soul:

भूमिरापोऽनलो वायुः खं मनो बुद्धिरेव च।

अहङ्कार इतीयं मे भिन्ना प्रकृतिरिष्टधा।।VII.4।।

अपरेयमतिस्त्वन्यां प्रकृतिं विद्धि मे पराम्।

जीवभूतां महाबाहो ययेदं धार्यते जगत्।।VII.5।।

" Earth, water, fire, air and ether, Manas, Buddhi and Ahankara thus eightfold is My manifestation. This is the lower, but other than this, known My higher manifestation which has become the Jiva, Oh, strong armed, by which (manifestation) this world is upheld." From this it follows that while all manifestations in the universe may be looked upon, from one standpoint of view as proceeding from the supreme soul without which they have no independent existence, these manifestations cannot be said to be a permanent property of that "Being" in as much as they do not always exist in it. This expressed by Sri Krishna in the following apparently paradoxical statements. " All beings dwell in Me, and I do not dwell in them; nr do beings swell in Me, behold My divine Yoga" (IX 4-5). Though this universal soul or Brahman is the only reality from a philosophic point of view, the word "real" cannot be said to fully describe it, for in common parlance we apply the term "real" to things that have a permanent existence in the wakeful state. If that which persists in the wakeful state is real, that which persists through all states of consciousness should be more than real. Of course unreal would be an evident misnomer for Brahman. Hence the Gita says :

ज्ञेयं यत्तत्प्रवक्ष्यामि यज्ज्ञात्वाऽमृतमश्नुतो
अनादिमत्परं ब्रह्म <u>नसत्तन्नासदुच्यते</u>।।XIII.13।।

"It is said to be neither real nor unreal."

The Brahman

In considering the nature of Kshetrajna, we are thus necessarily dragged to the consideration of the Brahman. Five slokas of the thirteenth chapter of the Gita give a description of the Brahman. We have merely referred to this passage in introductory chapter. It is now necessary to consider it at some length. This passage contains many assertions of it, adding any explanatory words or phrases that may be necessary.

अध्यात्मज्ञाननित्यत्वं तत्त्वज्ञानार्थदर्शनम्।
एतज्ज्ञानमिति प्रोक्तमज्ञानं यदतोन्यथा।।XIII.12।।
ज्ञेयं यत्तत्प्रवक्ष्यामि यज्ज्ञात्वाऽमृतमश्नुतो
अनादिमत्परं ब्रह्म न सत्तन्नासदुच्यते।।XIII.13।।
सर्वतः पाणिपादं तत्सर्वतोऽक्षिशिरोमुखम्।
सर्वतः श्रुतिमल्लोके सर्वमावृत्य तिष्ठति।।XIII.14।।
सर्वेन्द्रियगुणाभासं सर्वेन्द्रियविवर्जितम्।
असक्तं सर्वभृच्चैव निर्गुणं गुणभोक्तृ च।।XIII.15।।
बहिरन्तश्च भूतानामचरं चरमेव च।
सूक्ष्मत्वात्तदविज्ञेयं दूरस्थं चान्तिके च तत्।।XIII.16।।
अविभक्तं च भूतेषु विभक्तमिव च स्थितम्।
भूतभर्तृ च तज्ज्ञेयं ग्रसिष्णु प्रभविष्णु च।।XIII.17।।
ज्योतिषामपि तज्ज्योतिस्तमसः परमुच्यते

ज्ञानं ज्ञेयं ज्ञानगम्यं हृदि सर्वस्य विष्ठितम्।।XIII.18।।

"Though it has no form in truth, yet there is no form which appears independently of it. Hence it is described as having hands and feet on all sides, eyes, ears and faces everywhere. Indeed though nothing can be predicted of it, yet whatever we predicate of anything, can never exist separate from Brahman. In this sense, therefore it may be said to possess all properties. Being beyond space it cannot be located in any particular place, but yet whatever we see inside or outside exists only in Brahman, and so we might also say that it is, in essence , everywhere. Being the subtlest part of ourselves, it can never be said to be known; so it is very distant from the knowledge of ignorant, but being our very Self, it is nearer than the nearest and it is the only existence of which we can be emphatically confident. It is the one undivided reality in all being, though owing to extraneous forms of an unreal nature, it seems to be many and distinct. As nothing in the universe has an existence independent of Brahman, and is finally seen to be unreal when compared to it, the whole of the universe may be said to proceed from Brahman may be said to proceed from Brahman, exist in Brahman and return to Brahman. It is the light of light, for neither the sun nor the moon or the stars could shine of themselves without Brahman, while Brahman is self—luminous. Therefore it is beyond all darkness, for what darkness can ever enter into that which is ever luminous? In a word, what we call the means of knowledge is this Brahman, what we call the means of knowledge is also this Brahman is truth, and what we call knowledge, the result of knowing, is also really this Brahman. This Brahman is seated and can be realised in the heart of everyone that wishes to do so." Such is the Brahman, as described in the thirteenth chapter.

The use of Knowledge

We shall now consider the use of this knowledge. The first use will be that we shall get a sure basis of morality. It is often taught by religions that we should love our neighbor like ourselves. But why should we do so? This can be explained only in Jnana Yoga:

समं पश्यन्हि सर्वत्र समवस्थितिमीश्वरम्।

न हिनस्त्यात्मनाऽऽत्मानं ततो याति परां गतिम्।।XIII.29।।

" Seeing the same God residing everywhere, one does not injure self by self, and therefore reaches the highest goal." When man realises that his neighbor is his own self, how can he hate him?

"वद्यावनियसपंन्ने ब्राह्मणे गवि हस्तनिि।

शुनि चैव श्वपाके च पण्डितिा: समदर्शनि:॥V.18॥"

" The wise regard with which equal impartiality, a learned and well – behaved Brahman, a cow, an elephant, a dog and an outcaste."[8] The universal love exercised equally towards all beings will be the direct effect of knowledge. Knowledge supplies a good criticism of right and wrong. Whatever tends to unite beings to harmony, to Loka -Sangraha as the Gita puts it, is right. Whatever separates beings and tends to create discord is wrong. Jnana again enables a person to be inured to all external influences. Having learnt to identify himself with the Great Reality beyond the three Gunas constitute Prakriti, the Jnanin is secure against the influence of Gunas.

"न प्रहृष्येत्प्रियं प्राप्य नोद्विजेत्प्राप्य चाप्रियम्।

स्थिरबुद्धिरसम्मूढो ब्रह्मविद्ब्रह्मणि स्थिति:॥V.20॥

" The firm minded and ever watchful knower of Brahman taking stand in Brahman as he does, would not be puffed up with prosperity nor cast down by ill-fortune." Not that he avoids the world and its doings. He may mix with society how much fatiguing work, he will yet never lose sight of the one reality with which he has identified himself. He ever maintains Yoga or evenness of mind, in virtue of which he is never disturbed.

नैव किंचित्करोमीति युक्तो मन्यते तत्त्ववित्।

पश्यन् शृण्वन्स्पृशञ्जिघ्रन्नश्नन्गच्छन्स्वपन् श्वसन्॥V.8॥

प्रलपन्विसृजन्गृह्णन्नुन्मिषन्निमिषन्नपि।

इन्द्रियाणीन्द्रियार्थेषु वर्तन्त इति धारयन्॥V.9॥

" The knower of truth would consider himself as not acting at all in reality. Though apparently he is seeing, touching, smelling, eating, going, sleeping, breathing, weeping, leaving, taking, opening or shutting the eyes, ever noting that it is the senses that act on the sense objects." The Jnana Yogin alone can work best because he gets never attached to his work, and by his identification with the universal consciousness, has acquired the power of doing unimpassioned work. He incessantly works for harmony and at the same time ever keeps in view the principle that consciousness which is his real self, is above all actions. He is, in a word, in the world but not of it.

The necessity of Religious Practice to attain JNANA

Before we leave Jnana Yoga, it is quite easy for every one to say "I am by nature pure and blessed and above action," but to show this in practical life is very difficult. The Gita says:

आश्चर्यवत्पश्यति कश्चिदेन माश्चर्यवद्वदति तथैव चान्यः।

आश्चर्यवच्चैनमन्यः श्रृणोति श्रुत्वाप्येनं वेदं न चैव कश्चति।। II.29।।

"One man looks on this self as a marvel and so also another talks of it as a marvel, while a third man listens with equal wonder, but no one even having heard, know this(Atman) aright." The purity, blessedness and actlessness which are undoubtedly the birth – right of all, are in most of us, dimmed or evolved in darkness. We have by a series of self-hypnotic acts made ourselves impure, wretched, and action-bound. First we have forgotten the purity and self- effulgence of our real life, and then goaded on by all sorts of vain desires, we have converted ourselves into miserable worldlings.

धूमेनाव्रियते वह्निर्यथाऽऽदर्शो मलेन च।

यथोल्बेनावृतो गर्भस्तथा तेनेदमावृतम्।। III.38।।

"An ire is evolved in smoke, as a mirror is covered with dirt, as an embryo is covered with caul, so is this (knowledge) covered with that (desire)." So this knowledge though inherent in us, has to be discovered as it were afresh. Unless we get rid of the smoke, the scorching light of knowledge cannot shine forth; unless we polish the mirror and get rid of the accumulated dirt, knowledge cannot be reflected in our mind. Hence is the necessity for religious practices. These practices are not for creating anything new, but for polishing the mind. Merely reading books or hearing lectures or even sharp reasoning will be of noo use unless we polish the mirror first. As the Vivekachudamani says :

Description: I:\Geetai-Mission-2022\The Heart of The Bhagavadgita\Picture26.png

"Eloquence of speech, different ways of throwing words, as well as the learning of philosophies is for enjoyment not for freedom." The one thing necessary for freedom is self –culture or conquest of all selfishness.

तस्मात्त्वमिन्द्रियाण्यादौ नियम्य भरतर्षभ।

पाप्मानं प्रजहि ह्येनं ज्ञानविज्ञाननाशनम्।। III.41।।

" Therefore do thou first control the senses and then, Oh, best of Bharata's descendants, get rid of this evil of selfish desire which is the destroyer of wisdom theoretical and practical."

Hence the Gita enumerates a number of prerequisite of Jnana Yoga and concludes the list with the remark " This is true wisdom and what is other than this is ignorance." The list includes the following: --

" Humbleness, sincerity, non-injury, forbearance, rectitude, reverence for the teacher, purity, constancy, self—control, contempt of sense pleasure, self-sacrifice, thinking over the evil of birth, death, age, disease and suffering, non-attachment, absence of extreme attachment to children, wife, house and such things, an ever tranquil heart in fortunes good and fortunes evil; exclusive and faithful devotion to God, frequenting a quiet place for meditation, dissatisfaction with vulgar society preserving study of the science of Self and pondering over the knowledge of the Ultimate Reality." These requisites have been condensed into three by the Gita under the names Sraddha (faith), Tatparata (perseverance) and Samyatendriyata (control of the senses). We have already dwelt on these qualifications at the beginning of Jnana Yoga. It may be noticed here that the same qualifications are sometimes classed under four heads, by some Vedantic philosophers, "discrimination, renunciation, moral life and burning desire for freedom." Of the fourfold means we have already had occasion to remark elsewhere on renunciation at some length. Discrimination is ascertaining with the aid of right reason the real as distinguished from the unreal. This is in fact the knowledge of Kshetra and Kshetrajna, which has been the subject of the present section. Morality is the very life of religion. It will be noticed that these three requisites are not exclusive of one another and each can be well pursed only along with others. Indeed they may be said to be different aspects of the same thing. Again, these are not merely the means of knowledge, but they are the chief distinguishing marks of a perfect Jnana Yogin. They are not a sort of initial ordeal to be gone through for the sake of knowledge, but they are the permanent features of the perfectly illumined soul (Jnana-Nishtha).[9] In fact, discrimination, renunciation and morality reach their culmination only in such an ideal person. Hence no one can have too much of these indispensable spiritual qualifications. But none of these three are possible for a person without a genuine aspiration. Until this aspiration is born in our heart, religion has not begun for us. No one is fit to become a Jnanin until he is literally a philosopher, the lover of wisdom. This sentiment is voiced by Sri Krishna when he says :

अथ चित्तं समाधातुं न शक्नोषि मयि स्थिरम्।
अभ्यासयोगेन ततो मामिच्छाप्तुं धनञ्जय।। XII.9।।

"If you are unable to fix your mind exclusively on Me then desire to reach Me through the Yoga of practice, Oh, wealth—winner."

We shall take leave of this aspect of Yoga with a paradoxical quotation from the Gita.

या निशा सर्वभूतानां तस्यां जागर्ति संयमी।
यस्यां जाग्रति भूतानि सा निशा पश्यतो मुनेः।। II.69।।

"What is darkness to all other beings, in that the self –controlled is wide awake and that in which beings are awake is darkness to the seeing sage." If we classify persons into two classes, worldly and spiritual, we may say, that the worldly know nothing of the Ultimate Reality; they are quite in the dark so far as the truth of things is concerned. The spiritual person similarly lives in utter oblivion[10] of the world known to the vulgar, for his world is the world of truth. But a spiritual soul cannot be rightly said to know nothing of the ordinary world, for, he sees the utter hollowness of the world. By living oblivious of the world is not meant, retiring to a forest or cave, or to live away from society in some other manner. The Jnanin is ever present in society, looking at the eternal play of the Lord going on in the world and helps as far as he can to add to the merriment. In all he sees or does, however, he sees nothing but Brahman.

सङ्कल्पप्रभवान्कामांस्त्यक्त्वा सर्वानशेषतः।
मनसैवेन्द्रियग्रामं विनियम्य समन्ततः।।VI.24।।

" The offering is Brahman, the oblation is Brahman, in the fire which is Brahman is it poured by Brahman. Thus he whose instruments of Karma are all Brahman, must, of necessary, reach Brahman alone." Thus the Jnanin sees not only Brahman in all beings, he not only realises that the same readily indwells all beings in the world but also realizes Brahman in his divine ecstatic vision, in all feelings, actions, persons, in short, to him the whole creation becomes deified. He in fact sees nothing but Brahman. To such a person, therefore, Yoga is an accomplished fact. For, what is Yoga? "समत्वम् योग उच्च्यते" "Equanimity is Yoga." A Jnanin being one who sees Brahman everywhere, nothing can possibly upset his mind. The Jnanin displaces as it where all disturbing elements in nature by one homogeneous principle "equanimity."

इहैव तैर्जितः सर्गो येषां साम्ये स्थितं मनः।
निर्दोषं हि समं ब्रह्म तस्माद्ब्रह्मणि ते स्थिताः।। V.19 ।।

"Even in this life is nature conquered by those whose mind is firmly fixed on evenness, for Brahman is pure and everywhere the same, hence they live in Brahman."

[1] an ancient or modern philosopher who denies the possibility of knowledge, or even rational belief, in some sphere.

[2] Shankar Bhashya Sutras I – 1-1-2;

[3] Dr Paul Deussen: " The life a dream! This has been the thought of many wise men from Pindar and Sophocles to Shakspere and Calderson de la Barsa, but nobody has better explained the idea thau Sanskara (The Philosophy of the Vedanta, an address delivered before the Bombay Branch of the Royal Asiatic Society on 25-2-1893). "You see the concordance of Indian, Greek and German metaphysics ; the world is Maya, is illusion, says Sankara; - it is a world od shadows, not of realities, says Plato; - it is "appearance only, not the thing in itself," says Kant. In one of the later Upanishads, the श्वेताश्वतर

Description: I:\Geetai-Mission-2022\The Heart of The Bhagavadgita\Picture4.jpg

The notion, so prominent in the later system, that the material world is all illusion, is first met with. The world is here explained as an illusion produced by Brahman as a conjurer. This notion is, however, inherent even in the oldest Upanishads. It is virtually identical with the teachings of Plato that the things of experience are only the shadows of the real thing and with the teaching of Kant that they are only phenomena of the thing in itself." (pp. 221, Histoory of Sanskrit Literature, by Prof. A. A. Macdonell).

"To his (Mahomed's) eyes it is forever clear that this world wholly is miraculous. He said what all great thinkers, the rude Scandinavians themselves, in one way or the other, have contrived to see, that this so solid-looking material world is, at bottom, in very deed, Nothing, is a visual and tactual Manifestation of God's power and presence, a shadow hung-out by Him on the bosom of the void Infinite; nothing more." (Carlyle: on Heroes, Lecture II).

[4] Mr. Bal Gangadhar Tilak, in his recently published Marathi treatise on the Bhagavadgita called Bhagavad-gita-rahasya, construes the expression "ब्रह्मविद्यायां योगशास्त्रे" *as* "ब्रह्मविद्यान्तर्गत कर्मयोगशास्त्रे." *It will be shown, in the concluding remarks of the present work, that Mr. Tilak's interpretation is not correct.*

[5] functioning as plural) archaic cows; cattle;

[6] Sankara Bhashya, Bhagavdgita (III-20) "Loka Sangraha is preventing people from going astray from the right path."

[7] Causality, being an English term, (also referred to as causation, or combination cause and effect) is influence by which one event, process, state, execution or object (a cause) contributes to the formation of another event, process, execution, state, or object (an effect) where the cause will remain partly , or in some cases wholly, responsible for the effect, and the effect, in turn, remain partly or wholly dependent on the cause.

[8] Of course it would be ridiculous to interpret this verse literally, for n man, not to speak of a wise man, would think of making his external behavior the same to all men and beasts alike. our external behavior would be the same, viz., unbounded love.

[9] Where you find unbroken gentleness, enduring patience, sublime lowliness, graciousness of speech, self—control, self-forgetfulness and deep and abounding sympathy, look there for the highest wisdom, seek the company of such a one, for he has realized the divine, he lives with the Eternal, he has become one with the Infinite." (Ch XII, From Poverty to Power by James Allen).

[10] Oblivion meaning: the state of being unaware or unconscious of what is happening around one.

CHAPTER FOUR

Bhakti Yoga

Man's search after Happiness

In treating of Jnana Yoga we had occasion to remark that man's soul is originally pure and free and religion is the struggle to regain that freedom. We shall in the present section take up a special aspect of this freedom, viz, freedom from misery. Every being in the world shows by its activity the wish to reach a higher state, a dis-satisfaction with the present. Man is vividly conscious of a well-defined limitation to his powers of obtaining knowledge and enjoyment. The vast achievements of man from an immemorial past to the present day serve only to leave him impressed with the idea of an infinite region not yet conquered. This certainly of the possession of power, knowledge, and enjoyment is confined to a very narrow circle while doubt and darkness prevail as regards the outer skirts of that boundary. This knowledge of his own limitations in every way is the chief source of misery and all attempts of mankind may be described as conscious or unconscious trials in right or wrong directions to go beyond this boundary. In a word, man wants to reach eternal happiness and to avoid all misery.

The way out of Misery lies through BHAKTI

There have been two solutions of this problem of misery. One as propounded by a school of thinkers is that no doubt evil exists in this world but this evil is irremediable. So the best thing to do, is to make the best of it. To live as merely as we can, to snatch what pleasure we can and then to succumb to fate, this is the solution. this was the philosophy of the Charvakas of Ancient India, who said that all the Vedas were the invention of fools and cheats. Even in our times it is sometimes asserted that we ought to take the good and forget the evil as there is no help for it. But this is a piece of impracticable advice. Pleasures and pains make themselves felt in spite of efforts to ignore them. The world is a mixture of both. He lives in a fool's paradise, who thinks of making merry while conscious of unending misery. Thus we see that this solution is not very satisfactory. There is another solution of misery. This is the solution of religion. Religion says that we can take heart and march on. If we can only forget our little joys and artificial remedies of evil, we can go beyond this misery.

Description: I:\Geetai-Mission-2022\The Heart of The Bhagavadgita\Picture27.jpg

"The removal of this three –fold misery" is not possible by artificial means, for even after repression its recurrence is experienced," says the Sankhya sutra (I – 2). Religion therefore says that the way out of misery is not through artificial means. It lies through the help of a being who is eternally blissful, pure and free. We have seen how in man is implanted the double instinct of misery and happiness. Man is conscious of his misery – of his limited knowledge, existence and enjoyment – but at the same time, there is in him the never to be extinguished idea of lasting bliss. All men from the lowest savage to the most civilized person are full of this belief in a something which is infinite, knowledge, infinite existence and infinite bliss. This ingrained belief of man in the existence of the Infinite is undeniable. This ideal infinite is the God of religion. This may be explained away in some manner, but there it exists. The belief in God is not peculiar to the masses. Men illustrious in every field of scientific enquiry have affirmed their faith in this Being. Our purpose here is not to discuss the propriety of the belief, but to note that the belief exists in a very large proportion of mankind. Some people while they disclaim the belief yet postulate an existence and give it pet names of their own. We shall here include all these under the term God, God being the most comprehensive term as conveying all the different ideas. The absolute (Avyakta), the unchangeable (Akshara), the moral law (Dharma), the ultimate truth (Tattwa), existence (Sat), the beyond (Para), matter (Sara), ideal Unity (Eka), are some of the names. We have here noted against each name, a Sanskrit approximate translation, these terms being all taken out of the Gita and the Upanishads which apply all of them to God. Now, religion says that the way out of misery is through the help of this pure and perfect Supreme Being. Or rather this Being is perfect bliss and learning to love this God is the way out of misery. The Yoga which lays down principles of the art of developing and cultivating this love is called the Bhakti Yoga.

God according to Bhakti Yoga

So far as the Gita teachings are concerned it should be noted this God is not a mere conjencture, but the Highest Reality. For, God is the same as the Brahman we saw in Jnana Yoga. We there learnt how Brahman is the only Reality and also how everything in this world may be looked upon as a manifestation of Brahman. Now, God is the highest manifestation of Brahma, the highest reading of that Brahman by the human intellect. "ब्रह्मणो हि प्रतिष्ठाहम " (XIV.) " am indeed the abiding place of Brahman" says Sri Krishna. It is true also that other beings are manifestations but they are as it were only fractional manifestations.

ममैवांशो जीवलोके जीवभूत: सनातन:।

मन:षष्ठानीन्द्रियाणि प्रकृतिस्थानि कर्षति॥15.7॥

"My own part is manifested as the eternal Jiva in the world." To take a simile from Swami Vivekananda " The clay mouse can never become a clay elephant, because as manifestations, form alone makes them what they are, though as unformed clay they are all alone." As manifested beings then we are God's eternal slaves and worshippers. Through his worship, we are to go beyond this misery of life.

किं पुनर्ब्राह्मणा: पुण्या भक्ता राजर्षयस्तथा।

अनित्यमसुखं लोकमिमं प्राप्य भजस्व माम् ॥ IX.33॥

" As you have got into this transient and miserable life, worship Me. (IX – 33)."

The God of Bhakti Yoga, then is not different from the Good or Brahman of Jnana Yoga. It is the same God seen through the spectacles of love. Jnana Yoga says that God in his essence is beyond all predicates and hence to describe Him, it employs a negative language, "नसत्तन्नासदुच्यते" " It is neither real nor unreal" and so on. But Bhakti Yoga gives positive definitions of God. It is true that God is really infinitely more than the highest attributes known to human language; it is true that all attributes only delimit Him. But since all our words at best indicate or suggest this great reality, but can never directly and exactly signify it, is it not best to apply the best attributes our language can command? Our language is necessarily inaccurate, but why refrains from using the best expressions we have? The heart of man is ever declaring that there is a Being which is the embodiment of all knowledge, existence and bliss. This is supported by reason, which establishes that God is the highest manifestation of Brahman. And therefore Bhakti Yoga unhesitatingly applies the positive language:

त्वमादिदेवः पुरुष पुराण स्त्वमस्य विश्वस्य परं निधानम्।

वेत्तासि विद्यं च परं च धाम त्वया ततं विश्वमनन्तरूप।।11.38।।

"Thou art the Primeval Lord, the Ancient Person; thou art the great Hidden Treasure of the Universe; thou art the All – knowing and thou art the One to be known; (thou art) the highest abode, by thee is the universe pervaded, Oh, Omniformed One."

पितासि लोकस्य चराचरस्य त्वमस्य पूज्यश्च गुरुर्गरीयान्।

न त्वत्समोऽस्त्यभ्यधिकः कुतोऽन्यो लोकत्रयेऽप्यप्रतिमप्रभाव।।XI.43।।

"Thou art the father of this world animate and inanimate; thou art the One worthy of worship by this world; thou art the Great Teacher; there is not in all the triple world any one equal to thee, -- whence a greater? – incomparably mighty One as thou art." (XI- 43) "

The crossing of Maya or Spiritual Realisation

Bhakti Yoga as we have said is the search after the infinite bliss or God through love. All men are engaged in an unwearied search after an eternal object of love, a something which they can depend upon. All attempts are baffled but man continues in his endeavours. Is this not a sure sign that are certain of finding it sooner or later, if there be bliss at all in this universe? Sri Krishna vouchsafes in the following sloka that man's hope is not at all a dream, and going beyond misery is possible.

दैवी ह्येषा गुणमयी मम माया दुरत्यया।

मामेव ये प्रपद्यन्ते मायामेतां तरन्ति ते। VII.14।।

" This My Divine Maya made of Gunas, is difficult to cross; whosoever seek refuge with Me alone, they cross this Maya. (VII- 14)." When a person hearkens to this advice, and consciously strives to take refuge with the Lord, he has begun to tread the field of Bhakti Yoga. Maya in this sloka refers to nature where the interplay of the three Gunas is manifested. God can properly call Maya "Mine" for He is ever the master of the three Gunas and keeps them under control. But for other souls, Maya is like a boundless ocean, very difficult to cross without an aid. Trusting ourselves to the Great Pilot, we can safely find ourselves on the other side of the deep.

There is another beautiful metaphysical representation of the idea, in the Bhagavadgita :

ईश्वरः सर्वभूतानां हृद्देशेऽर्जुन तिष्ठति।
भ्रामयन्सर्वभूतानि यन्त्रारूढानि मायया।।18.61।।

" The Lord is seated in the heart of all beings, Oh, Arjuna, turning round by means of Maya all beings who are mounted on the merry-go-round world." There is a reference here to the merry-go-round which consists of painted horses and other animals (of wood) moved round by a mechanical contrivance. Persons are seated on these artificial animals and are allowed to wheel, a number of rounds of this mock-ride. This world, says the Gita, is a huge magical mechanism of this kind. God is the Manager, our bodies and possessions are the animals on which we ride. As the machine is turned round and round, the animals fly in the air, faster and faster at various heights. One is high and another is low, and the fun goes on. But to enjoy this fun it is necessary to seat ourselves firm and to keep up the balance aright so that we may not fall. Sometimes we forget that we are merely playing, and taking it seriously we are sometimes tempted to think with pride "How high I have risen above my neighbour!" This very pride and carelessness, however, is the cause of our downfall and takes away the pleasure of the whole play. Pride goeth before a fall, as the proverb says; to avoid this foolish pride and to learn to take pleasure consciously it is necessary to keep up the balance. This balance is possible only when we hit upon the centre of gravity, which is God. We cannot enjoy the fun unless we seek refuge with the Lord of the play.

It is necessary here, to meet an objection which is sometimes taken about the theory of Maya and Sport. It is thought a low and unworthy conception of the Deity to have a Maya in which souls get entangled. The view degrades the Supreme Being, which makes Him "moved by such a sportive and unmeaning impulse"[1] as creation. This view of creation, that it is a mere sport, is considered to militate against "the claim of Theism that the creation is due to a motive on the part of Brahman that moves Him to reveal Himself." Leaving aside all philosophical views of creation for a while one is yet unable to conceive how it is derogatory to Godhead to have arranged for an eternal game of merriment and to have expected the souls to participate in the joy thereof. If it is admitted that it is the essence of God to reveal himself, and if it is taken for granted, likewise that this desire of self-communication, is the motive for creation (these two being postulates of all cosmological theories of theology), then in what manner should we expect the Deity to manifest Himself? In a way to be understood, loved and enjoyed by souls or in a way to be feared, estranged from all hearts and hated by all? To make the creation a playground or to make it a hell? It is no sin, therefore, to hold that the creation is a kind of play. Even games are regularly planned and carried out. A play would be no play if it were not played according to fixed rules. God in his infinite mercy, has arranged this play for us. God is not making fun of our vain struggles and desires. The struggles and desires are obstacles to the play thrown by ourselves. Whether we go high or low, as we ride on our mock-horses, we should neither feel proud nor be cast down, for that would destroy the fun. We should only enjoy the play. " If you are poor enjoy that as fun; if you are rich enjoy the fun of being rich; if dangers come, treat them also as fun; if happiness comes, there is more good fun."[2] So much for the sport of divine creation. As for Maya it is no blank magic wrought by a jealous being to entice human souls into misery. It has been observed that the s'loka just quoted says it is made up of Gunas. Maya is another name of Prakriti or nature, and nature is, as we have elsewhere remarked, neither good nor bad. It is a mixture of good and bad, and these terms good and bad are only relative so that no one thing in nature can be said to be good or bad in itself. To make the world or Maya, good or bad, depends entirely on ourselves. The Gita says Maya can be thus mastered and the world converted into beautiful heaven of bliss. "They who resort to Me alone cross this Maya," says Sri Krishna.

Theimportance of the Education of the Heart

The s'loka we last quoted says that the Lord is seated in the heart of all beings and we are asked to take refuge in the Lord. We should understand this to mean that the cultivation of the heart is the most necessary step for spiritual realisation. There is no religion in the world, which does not advocate the roper training of that art of the human mind which is properly known as the heart. Intellectual investigations are most necessary to clear the understanding, and to make our belief firm. But it should not be forgotten, that intellect by itself achieves nothing. It is like a lame person who talks from where he is seated. The work of the intellect is always negative, for it can only remove errors and false beliefs. On the other hand, what are called our emotions and feelings are more daring. There is no region which they have not the curiosity to explore. But the heart by itself is like a half blind person, who by willfully making where he lists, falls times without number into ditches and is miserably bruised. But by mutual help, intellect and feelings may be so combined as to produce the most beneficent results and avoid all unnecessary pit-falls and dangers. It is this happy combination in a more or less degree that has produced the world's great men. Speaking from a religious point of view, however, one is inclined to think, that on the whole it is far better to have a little feeling even without a good intellect rather than to have a highly developed head without heart. It is through feelings that one will see the Lord, and the training of feelings in the right way is the special providence of Bhakti Yoga. Hence, who is qualified to enter upon a course of Bhakti? It is the man of feelings. Bhakti Yoga does not impose conditions of birth, sex, occupation, wealth, power or learning. Sri Krishna says

मां हि पार्थ व्यपाश्रित्य येऽपि स्युः पापयोनयः।

स्त्रियो वैश्यास्तथा शूद्रास्तेऽपि यान्ति परां गतिम्॥ IX.32॥

" Those that depend on Me even if they be of ignoble birth, - women, Vais'yas (merchants) or S'udras (laborers), even they will attain the highest goal." The one and only pre-requisite is feeling and a desire to improve feeling.

The transformation of ordinary Love into Bhakti

Of course everyone has feelings and emotions but they are generally in a most neglected condition, being least developed and exercised always in the wrong direction. Still no one need despair, how deplorable so ever the condition of his heart may be.

अपि चेत्सुदुराचारो भजते मामनन्यभाक्।

साधुरेव स मन्तव्यः सम्यग्व्यवसितो हि सः॥ IX.30॥

क्षिप्रं भवति धर्मात्मा शश्वच्छान्तिं निगच्छति।

कौन्तेय प्रतिजानीहि न मे भक्तः प्रणश्यति॥ IX.31॥

"Even if a highly impious person loves Me exclusively, he must be deemed a good man, for he is wisely resolved; soon he becomes a virtuous soul and attains eternal peace. You may be sure, Oh, son of Kunti, My devotee is not ruined (ix- 30,31)" says Bhagavan. Once with a desire to self-improvement we begin to attend to our feelings, we soon get Bhakti. In fact, our feelings developed, regulated and properly directed, become Bhakti.

Bhakti Yoga then chiefly aims at converting ordinary love into Bhakti of God love. To find the Lord through love is the most natural method as we have already remarked, for man is miserable and wants happiness. We find misery in objects of hatred and pleasure, in objects of love, and there it follows that infinite happiness must be in that which is the eternal object of the highest love. The problem of the religious aspirants is, according to the view, therefore reduced to the simple one of the finding such an object. Among all the means to salvation, accordingly, Bhakti Yoga holds love in the fore-front rank.

नाहं वेदैर्न तपसा न दानेन न चेज्यया।

शक्य एवंविधो द्रष्टुं दृष्टवानसि मां यथा।। XI.53।।

"Sri Krishna says "Neither by Vedas nor by asceticism, neither by charity nor by sacrifice is it possible to see Me in the manner thou hast done, but by exclusive devotion, it is possible to know Me like this, to see Me in truth and be assimilated into Me. (XI- 53)" In the study of Bhakti Yoga, it is therefore important to note that higher (Para) Bhakti or God Love is but the same feeling as the lower (Gouni) love with a difference of direction. Just as by judicious manipulation harmful reuse and filth may be converted into useful manure for the orchard, just as useless and foul smelling parts of animals can be dexterously manufactured into useful articles of daily use, and just as even poisons by scientific compounding can be turned not only into harmless but also into potent medicines, so by Bhakti Yoga, a process is offered byy means of which all our lower passions are made to work out our salvation. It is in this that the naturalness of Bhakti Yoga lies.

Love in its lowest forms

To study how this method works, we should consider love from its lowest stage up to the stage when it becomes Bhakti. In its lowest form, love is called KAMA or desire and lust. It is then the greatest impediment to spiritual progress. All religions have preached against covetousness and evil passion, and the Gita is no less vehement in its condemnation of these feelings. When Arjuna asked Sri Krishna who it was that moved the soul to sin, he perhaps implied that God or some supernatural Being was compelling man to go wrong. He said,

अथ केन प्रयुक्तोऽयं पापं चरति पूरुषः।

अनिच्छन्नपि वार्ष्णेय बलादिव नियोजितः।। III.36।।

"But by whom induced does this man commit sin, Oh, descendant of Vrishni, being urged on, as it were by force even against his will? (III- 36)" S'ri Krishna to show emphatically that man is not compelled by any external force and that evil is his own free choice, replied in the following words:

काम एष क्रोध एष रजोगुणसमुद्भवः।

महाशनो महापाप्मा विद्ध्येनमिह वैरिणम्।। III.37।।

"This is desire, this is wrath, born of the primal Guna of Rajas greatly voracious and immensely harmful, know this to be the foe here. (III – 37)" what is called sin, therefore, is the direct outcome of such desire or lust. This low desire disappointed becomes anger, and when fulfilled results in fond attachment and miserliness. Hence the Gita elsewhere says:

त्रिविधं नरकस्येदं द्वारं नाशनमात्मनः।

कामः क्रोधस्तथा लोभस्तस्मादेतत्त्रयं त्यजेत्।।XVI.21।।

एतैर्विमुक्तः कौन्तेय तमोद्वारैस्त्रिभिर्नरः।

आचरत्यात्मनः श्रेयस्ततो याति परां गतिम्।। XVI.22।।

"Three fold is this doorway to hell, which destroys the soul; (it is made up of) desire, anger, and miserliness, and therefore one should avoid these three. A man free from these three gets to darkness, Oh, son of Kunti, acts for his good and therefore reaches the highest goal. (XVI – 21- 22)." In the view of the Gita, therefore, the one original source of all errors of the human mind, is this love in its lowest form desire. Desire takes a number of forms. The Brihadaranyakopanishad says,

"कामः संकल्पो विचिकित्सा श्रद्धाऽश्रद्धा

धृतिरधृतिर्ह्री र्धीः भीरित्येतत् सर्वं मनः एव।।"

"Desire, will, doubt, faith, disbelief, firmness, frailty, modesty, thinking, fear, all such are verily the mind." From the standpoint under consideration, all these functions of the mind may be looked upon as aspects of love in which various degrees and stages of development. The lowest stage is, as said above, desire or sensuality. Desire, then, is the result of ignorant non-use or conscious misuse of love. The misuse of love makes man of a demonical nature. The sixteenth chapter of the Gita gives in about a dozen couplets an illustrative description of this nature, there called ASURI SAMPAT (wealth of demons). One thing that is made prominent throughout the description is an inordinate love of body and a selfish love of wealth, wife and children. Love in this stage besides being called Karma (desire) sometimes also receives the name of Sanga (attachment). The difference in significance between the two words is this, that while Kama is desire for objects not attained, Sanga is attachment to things in possession. Now, in desire and attachment, men instead of giving as much room as possible for the free play of love, try to concentrate in on trivial and frivolous objects. This is the very reason of the soul's misery. By desiring various objects which are to be obtained only with great difficulty and which if obtained are sure soon to perish, man becomes the slave of his desires. His peace of mind is always disturbed by desires, and ne can never know anything of real happiness. Again by extreme attachment to the body and possession, man loses his independence and becomes a mere appendage to his belongings. Thus instead of the body belonging to the man, the man belongs to the body. Desire and attachment are the real bondage, for man totally surrenders his independence when he becomes subject to these feelings. On the other hand infinite peace belongs to him who can help himself above desires and attachment.

आपूर्यमाणमचलप्रतष्ठिं समुद्रमाप: प्रवशिन्ति यद्वत्।

तद्वत्कामा य प्रवशिन्ति सर्वे स शान्तिमाप्नोति न कामकामी।। II.70।।

"As the stream enters the sea which is constantly filled on all sides and yet stands unmoved, so into whom-so-ever enter all desires (without affecting him) he attains ease and not the man who has all sorts of desires. (II- 70)" So long, therefore, as we cherish this desire or abnormal love, we can never know anything of spiritual rest. Unending misery is the lot of all selfish persons. Hence to taste of spiritual bliss, it is absolutely necessary to give up this demon-like habit and to cultivate the divine accomplishment. "दैवी संपदवमिोक्षाय नबिाधा यासूरी मता. " " Godliness makes for freedom, but for bondage is the demonical held to be."

The Principle of the Renunciation of Low Desires

But how are we to give up this selfish habit which has become, as it were, our second nature? It is easy to say, "Give up desire and attachment" but to bring this into practice is extremely difficult. The Gita states a principle which offers the best solution here:

वषिया वनिविर्तन्त नरिाहारस्य देहनि: |

रसवर्ज रसोऽप्यस्य पर दष्ट्वा नविर्तत ||II 59||

" Objects are removed from the embodied being who does not take them in (through the senses), but not so the love of objects; even love is removed after having seen the highest (love)." Love of one object can be removed only when placed our love on something else. We are all trying to fix our love on something permanent, but do not succeed. For a moment we love an object and when we begin to attach under importance to it, when we think that there is no other object worthy of our love, the object is suddenly removed from us. Then we direct our love to something else. Or even while the object remains, we may take to another object as more worthy of our attainment. This shifting of love from object to object is the very force that moves all beings to action. In the words of Manu,

"यद्यपि किरुतं जन्तुततुततकामस्य वेष्टतिम" " Whatever a being does, that is the work of love." All beings are in a blindfold race, as ir were, towards some objects on which they want to fix their love permanently. We give up the lower love when we realise the higher love, for the quality and permanence of happiness depends both upon the sort of love and the objects loved. In the animals love is fixed on the objects grossest of pleasures. Love of sense pleasure of the grossest type predominates in these beings. But as man becomes more and more civilized even the sense pleasure become more and more refined and at last man finds out a higher love. Love is now placed in intellectual pleasures and lower pleasures lose their attraction. Love of morality is still a higher stage. Therefore, we may say greater and greater happiness is realised, as love becomes finer and finer. The finer love is taken up in preference to the grosser, and the latter naturally disappears. Therefore, says the gita, when the highest love is reached, all other forms of love are thrown into the shade and discharged.

God is Love

And what is the object of the highest love? It is a little peculiar that the line which man's selfishness takes should point out this object, to the utter annihilations of selfishness itself. Man loves things external to himself less than himself. The nearer the object of love to him, the more he loves. This principle stretched to its utmost limit leads us to the conclusion that nothing is more loveable than that which is the very self of us all; for, what can be nearer to us than our self? So we see that the search of love takes the same direction as the direction of knowledge. In fact, knowledge of a thing increases with the love of knowing it. It follows therefore, that the highest knowledge of the Lord comes to those that cherish the highest love for the Lord. In Jnana Yoga it was said that knowledge reaches its acme, when it realises the one supreme reality in all. Now, love is the best means of realising this, for whatever object we intensely love, we become identified with it for the time being. Thus when we love the body, the body is our self and for the lover of body there is no truth higher than it. When we love the mind, mind is our self, and there is nothing higher than it. In every case, everything else exists in and through the self and everything is loveable for the sake of the self, whatever we take the self to be for the time being. Love therefore always makes for the realisation of unity. When love learns by experience that no object can satisfy it, that no object can permanently engage it, it at last transforms itself, as it were, and turns back on its own real self. This is no doubt a yet difficult feat, but when performed, permanent bliss is reached. It is then found that the reality which is in the entire world is one and the same and its nature is perfect love. The essence, the reality, of love is love, and hence love can never hate love. All misery being the result of hatred disappears when love reaches this stage. Thus, after a weary search man finds that there is no object worthy of his love greater than the Lord, the Love seated in the heart of all. He then understands the meaning of the Narada Sutra "अनर्विचननीयम पूरेम सतूरम " " The nature of love is inexpressible." After one has seen this Paramarasa (Highest Love), all his lower love vanishes like a mirage.

For one reason Love is the greatest name that could be devised to indicate the Great Self. We have seen in the last section that one definition of Kshetrajna is "The knower of Kshetra." And that the Kshetra includes not only the external body but also the mind and all its functions such as desire and hatred. We have observed again in the present chapter that the chief functions of the mind such as desire may be considered to be different phases of love. Now, the mind is the nearest to the self, and the more it is purified, the more shines through it the self behind. Indeed, the mind and the self are so intimately connected that the mind is very often mistaken for the self. Sri Sankaracharya speaking of this confounding the self with the mind says "The mind is the illuminated and the light of the self is the illuminator like the ordinary light. Not distinguishing the illuminator and the illuminated is very common. For, being pure, light seems similar to the illuminated object. Thus while illuminating a red thing it seems similar to the red thing and assumes a red form. And illuminating green, black or brown thing, the light becomes similar to them. In the same way the self-illuminating the mind, illuminates the whole of Kshetra through the mind." (Brih. Bha) The Gita expresses this idea in the following text:

यथा प्रकाशयत्येकः कृत्स्नं लोकमिमं रविः।
क्षेत्रं क्षेत्री तथा कृत्स्नं प्रकाशयति भारत।।XIII.34।।

"Just as the one sun illuminates the whole of this world, so also the whole of Kshetra the Kshetrin illuminates, Oh, descendant of Bharata." The mind therefore being the nearest, catches as it were, the best reflection of the self. Since as we have said above, the supreme self is seen the more clearly, the more the mind is purified, it follows that the self as it is, can be seen only by the most purified mind. Now, the mind is most purified when all its lower passions are transformed into divine love or Bhakti. Since the highest truth shines forth only in the highest mind of love, is it not most appropriate to call it by the unique name of Love? Hence the Upanishad declares:

"रसो वै सः। रसं ह्येवायं लब्ध्वानन्दी भवति। को ह्येवान्यात् कः प्राण्यात्। यदेष आकाश आनन्दो न स्यात्।एष ह्येवानन्द यातायिदा ह्येवैष एतस्मिन्निदश्यऽनात्म्यऽनिरुक्तऽनिलयनऽभयं प्रतिष्ठां विन्दतो.........।"

""He is verily sweet love. Having got this Love alone, indeed, this soul becomes blissful."

Preparatory Bhakti

But until the mind is thoroughly purified, this Supreme Love is not realised.

न मां दुष्कृतिनो मूढाः प्रपद्यन्ते नराधमाः।
माययापहृतज्ञाना आसुरं भावमाश्रिताः।। VII.15।।

"The sinful, the ignorant, the lowest of men do not come to me, for their knowledge is removed through Maya, and they have taken to the demonaical life. (VII – 15)." Till supreme Bhakti is attained, therefore, a preparation towards that stage is necessary. The Gita divides seekers after truth into four classes.

चतुर्विधा भजन्ते मां जनाः सुकृतिनोऽर्जुन।
आर्तो जिज्ञासुरर्थार्थी ज्ञानी च भरतर्षभ।। VII.16।।

"Righteous person of four sorts worship Me, Oh, Arjuna; (they are) the afflicted, the enquiring, the interested, and the enlightened. (VII- 16)" these four classes are again brought under two main heads " Of these the best is the enlightened person whose mind is constantly applied and exclusively devoted to Me; for I am greatly beloved of the enlightened man, and he is also my beloved. All these are noble, indeed, but the enlightened man, is My very self, for by constant attachment, he holds on too Me as the highest goal

तेषां ज्ञानी नित्ययुक्त एकभक्तिर्विशिष्यते।

प्रियो हि ज्ञानिनोऽत्यर्थमहं स च मम प्रियः।। VII.17।।

उदारा: सर्व एवैते ज्ञानी त्वात्मैव मे मतम्।

आस्थितः स हि युक्तात्मा मामेवानुत्तमां गतिम्।।7.18।।

" It is clear from these texts that the three classes of Bhaktas (devotees) other than the Jnanin, are in the preparatory stage of Bhakti. But even preparatory Bhakti is not easily got, for they are qualified as the righteous (सुकृतिनः) in contradistinction to vicious or demonaical persons.

The Gita does not explain which of the three preparatory devotees is the best, but in Narada Bhakti Sutra, it is said that of the three each is preferable to the one immediately following it (in the above enumeration), whene it follows that according to this view the best preparatory approximation to the highest form of Bhakti is ARTA BHAKTI or to become conscious of the misery of Samsara and to resort to the Lord with whole-heartedness to be relieved of this distress. This is supported by the s'loka already quoted from the Gita: "Those who resort to Me alone, they cross the Maya." Initiatory to this stage are all other endeavours to purify the mind.

Purification of the Mind

Means of mind purification are three – fold according to the Gita,

यज्ञदानतप:कर्म न त्याज्यं कार्यमेव तत्।

यज्ञो दानं तपश्चैव पावनानि मनीषिणाम्।। XVIII.5।।:

"Sacrifice, charity and asceticism are all purifiers."

Sacrifice is of different kinds varying from the grossest worship with various materials to the highest worship in spirit and truth. Sacrifice is described at length in the fourth chapter. The best sacrifice is, according to the Gita, that which is done for its own sake (XVII – 11). The best charity is thus defines

दातव्यमिति यद्दानं दीयतेऽनुपकारिणो

देशे काले च पात्रे च तद्दानं सात्त्विकं स्मृतम् ।। XVII.20।।

" Charity given, just because it ought to be given, given without expectation of any return, in the right place, at the right time, and to the right persons – that charity is considered to be the best." As for Tapas or asceticism the Gita divides it into three classes, physical, verbal and mental. "Worship of God, the spiritual teacher and the wise man, purity, rectitude, chastity, harmlessness are said to be bodily Tapas. Unwounding, true, pleasant and agreeable speaking, and study of holy books, are said to be

Tapas of speech; clearness of mind, gentleness, studied silence, self-control, purity of heart- this is said to be the Tapas of the mind (XVII- 14-16) " These three –fold exercises done with intense faith and without expectation of reward constitute the best asceticism according to Gita according to the Gita (XVIII- 6-7).

In this preparatory Bhakti, which has been called Gouni by ancient writers, all such forms and symbols as are conducive to speedy realisation of divine love may be advantageously used. Some people are disposed to think that the use of symbols, forms, or other concrete helps is useless and even dangerous, inasmuch as these concrete things turn away the seeker's attention from God. They say that to recommend their use is to recommend a conscious alliance with falsehood and direct propagation of lies. But the Gita does not agree with such men. It is assumed here that as the use of formulae and symbols in science tends to only greater clearness of understanding, the use of symbols and forms is of great use in heling young minds to realise the true nature of worship. All great religions of the world having made use of symbols and forms to some extent at least, the Gita does not stand alone in the recommendation of such helps.

यो यो यां यां तनुं भक्तः श्रद्धयार्चितुमिच्छति।

तस्य तस्याचलां श्रद्धां तामेव विदधाम्यहम्।। VII.21।।

"Whatever devotee wishes to worship whatever form with faith I confirm his faith in the same." These forms and symbols must be worshipped not for their own sake but for the Lord. When used as a suggestion of God, they are not only beneficial but also necessary for all who are in the preparatory stage. But when the image, form or symbol is worshipped for its own sake, that is when it represents a saint or an angel or some being other than God, the worship has merits of its own, but cannot directly lead to real Bhakti (devotion to God) or Mukti (freedom). Hence the Bhakti says of such kind of Worship:

अन्तवत्तु फलं तेषां तद्भवत्यल्पमेधसाम्।

देवान्देवयजो यान्ति मद्भक्ता यान्ति मामपि।। VII.23।।

"But perishable is their reward, and it comes only to small wits." But even this little perishable result comes from the Lord:

येऽप्यन्यदेवता भक्ता यजन्ते श्रद्धयान्विताः।

तेऽपि मामेव कौन्तेय यजन्त्यविधिपूर्वकम्।। IX.23।।

" Even the devotees of the other Devatas who worship with faith, they are really worshipping Me in an indirect manner." Therefore to take the assistance of symbols and forms, and consciously worship the one Lord in them, is highly beneficial and recommendable. Such substitute or suggestions as it were, of God are stated at length in the tenth chapter of the Gita under name (विभूति) Vibhutis. It is interesting to observe how the Gita makes such Vibhutis, the stepping-stone to realisation of Bhakti or the love of one God. To begin with Sri Krishna states:

अहमात्मा गुड़ाकेश सर्वभूताशयस्थितः।

अहमादिश्च मध्यं च भूतानामन्त एव च॥ X.20॥

"I am the self, Oh, self- controlled, seated in the heart of all beings, I am the beginning, the middle and the end of begins." Then for such as may not understand this grand ideal, several approximations are given again at the end of the enumeration, a general statement is made

यद्यद्विभूतिमित्सत्त्वं श्रीमदूर्जितमेव वा।

तत्तदेवावगच्छ त्वं मम तेजोंऽशसंभवम्॥ X.41॥

"Whatever is magnificent, abundant and vigorous, know thou, that is born of a part of My own glory." Thus whatever is awe-inspiring, wonderful and admirable in nature and whoever represents goodness, greatness and wisdom are here recommended to be revealed in order that the heart may be gradually led to a sense of the One Infinite Being. From curiosity to fear, from fear to wonder, from wonder to admiration and from admiration to reverence and love; these are the various steps that the soul will take in its onward progress, and this progress will be speedy and well-directed just to the extent to which it can draw inspiration from the divine Vibhutis, viz., the Vedas, the Guru and the Avataras. The Bhagavadgita in its enumeration of Vibhutis is only illustrative and is by no means exhaustive, for Sri Krishana says,

नान्तोऽस्ति मम दिव्याना विभूतीना परंतप।

एष तूद्देशतः प्रोक्तो विभूतेर्विस्तरो मया॥ X.40॥

"There is no end to My Divine Vibhutis, Oh, tormentor of foes, but this list of Vibhutis, has been given by Me just in illustration." If the Gita names certain books, certain teachers and certain incarnations, it is merely because they were the best known to India of those times. If Krishna were to teach a modern world, we should not be surprised to hear him include the Dhammapada, the Bible, the Koran and the Zendavesta among sacred books, and Jesus, Mohammad, Zoroaster and Buddha among persons to be recored as manifestations. The perfectly general character of the teachings in the book warrants this supposition. Sri Krishna says:

ये यथा मां प्रपद्यन्ते तांस्तथैव भजाम्यहम्।

मम वर्त्मानुवर्तन्ते मनुष्या: पार्थ सर्वश:॥ IV.11॥

" whoever takes refuge with Me in whatever form, I take them into My service in that form; men follow My path, Oh, Son of Pritha, by all means." The Bhagavadgita therefore, cannot be justly held to advocate reverence to a particular book, teacher or divine incarnation. The book simply refers to the principle of Vibhutis and stops there. With these preliminary remarks, we shall now turn to a consideration of what the Gita has to say on each of these three Vibhutis. First of all, sacred gooks if rightly used are a great aid to the cultivation of religious feeling. Hence the Gita says,

तस्माच्छास्त्रं प्रमाणं ते कार्याकार्यव्यवस्थितौ।

ज्ञात्वा शास्त्रविधानोक्तं कर्म कर्तुमिहार्हसि॥ XVI.24॥

"Therefore the scriptures are your authority in distinguishing right and wrong." But it is necessary here to observe that we are not here given over to books bound hand and foot, for in a subsequent chapter, it is said that even persons without a scriptural authority are to be considered Satwic as if they work in good faith. As for teachers, the Gita gives them two epithets " (ज्ञानिन:) JNANINAH" "(तत्त्वदर्शिन:) TATWADARSSHINAH" "Possessed of knowledge" and "seers of truth." This is but a paraphrase of the Upanishad which says that the Guru must be S'rotriya and Brahmanishtha (Mundaka I- 2-12). The sure test of a genuine teacher is when knowledge is kindled and all confusion is vanished in the disciple's soul (IV- 35). The effect of the teaching must enable the taught to conquer all sin, to burn all evil tendencies, and to attain purity of spirit (IV – 36, 37). Now, for the Avataras; the Gita says that there will be Avataras again and again

परित्राणाय साधूनां विनाशाय च दुष्कृताम्।

धर्मसंस्थापनार्थाय संभवामि युगे युगे॥ IV.8॥

" Age after age I incarnate Myself for the establishment of religion" says S'ri Krishna. Whenever religion subsides and irreligion prevails, there will be an Avatara (IV-7). Besides showing that the purpose of Avatara is always moral, the Gita says that Avatara necessitates no limitations to God's self-sufficiency "Though without birth and of an undecaying nature, and the Lord of beings, I, controlling My Prakriti manifest Myself through My Maya" (IV–6). Hence the Gita never attaches too much importance to any particular Avataras, for it declares that all Avataras are for the upholding of religion. This is quite enough we think as a refutation of the theory that has been advanced by some, that the Gita is intended to revive the

Krishnavatara, and to advocate Krishna worship. In the whole of the Gita there is not single text betraying any jealousy of the worship of any other incarnation. On the other hand, all forms of worship are positively commended and given their right position in the ladder of spiritual progress. The Gita manifestly rests on the foundations of religion not on the infallibility of a book, nor on the authority of ceremonies, but on the right exercise of reasons and righteousness of conduct and on universal love, joy and peace. But at the same time the Gita is never antagonistic to any form, ceremony, book or person that may help souls in their onward march to spirituality. They are Vibhutis and may be justly revered. The Gita only wants to advise that instead of taking the Vibhuti for itself , it is infinitely more beneficial to take it as a symbol or suggestion of Lord who is revealed in it. That this is the object of the enumeration of Vibhutis is clear from the following concluding verse:

अथवा बहुनैतेन किं ज्ञातेन तवार्जुन।

विष्टभ्याहमिदं कृत्स्नमेकांशेन स्थितो जगत्॥ X.42॥

"Or, what is the good to you of knowing all this detail, Oh, Arjuna? Pervading the whole universe I stand revealed therein in part." Thus Vibhuti worship is meant to gradually take the soul upward and widen the aspirant's heart more and more till it enbraces the whole creation. The realisation will be complete, when the seeker has actualized that the Lord in His glory is infinitely revealed in the universe.

The method of Bhakti Yoga (in brief)

Before we proceed further it seems necessary, for clearness of understanding, to recapitulate the methods of Bhakti Yoga we have here and there alluded to in the preceding pages. First, the special aim of Bhakti Yoga being spiritual realisation, it does not at all attaché much importance to speculation, though right reasoning is not excluded from its sphere. Secondly, the education of the heart is its chief business, and its central secret is to give a nobler and a higher direction to our feelings and to transform them all into one intense religious feeling of supreme love. Thirdly, in its preparatory stage, Bhakti allows the use of forms, symbols and other helps to worship. Fourthly, all this must be made subservient to the one object of the realisation of the Lord who is manifested in the universe and who in His essence is infinitely more besides. Lastly, we note that in Bhakti Yoga, it is the personal aspect of God, that is chosen. The soul is here advised to escape from misery through the help of Is'wara or personal God. The impersonal aspect is not denied, but the personal alone is preferred for worship as being natural and ease of access. While Jnana Yogi takes up the impersonal and tries to tackle the problem of life mainly through philosophy, Bhakti Yoga recognises that the majority of mankind is unable to guide their lives by philosophy. Men often thinking themselves to be capable of scaling the heights of philosophy, suffer from great falls. To avoid this Bhakti Yoga offers a natural, smooth and gentle path. Sri Krishna says:

मय्यावेश्य मनो ये मां नत्यिय्ययुक्ता उपासतो।

श्रद्धया परयोपेतास्ते मे युक्ततमा मताः॥ XII.2॥

"Those who concentrating their mind on Me worship Me with eternal constancy and with the highest faith, they are, in my opinion, the best Yogis." That this refers to the personal aspect of God will be evident from the next three s'lokas where S'ri Krishna says, " But those that worship the Unchangeable, the Indescribable, the Un-manifested, the Omnipresent, the Unthinkable, the All-comprehending, the Immovable and the eternal, by controlling all their senses and having the conviction of equanimity with regard to all things, in doing good to all beings. But the difficulty is greater for those whose minds are devoted to the Un-manifested, for the path of the Un-manifested, is trodden indeed with great difficulty by embodied beings." Here the description is clearly with reference to the impersonal aspect. Hence the first one must be the personal God of Bhakti-Yoga. Bhakti then is best developed when it is directed to the personal aspect of God.

In the above quotation, a statement calls for some remark. It is said there that the way to the un-manifested is beset with difficulty for the embodied. Since all human beings have a body, does this mean that no man can worship the Absolute? This conclusion being plainly repugnant, the word embodied is better interpreted when it is made to mean those who are too much attached to the body. Many of us find it difficult to shake off the body idea. Many of us find it difficult to shake off the body idea. People often make the body everything. For such being, evidently, it is extremely difficult to go at once to the path of the highest philosophy which says that the world including the body is unreal. For all ordinary men, therefore, the worship of the personal is the only thing that is recommendable.

It must not be supposed, however, that the manifested God is a low existence, the worship of which is meant only for beginners as being easy enough. That would be the greatest mistake to commit about the Gita teaching in the matter. For, Sri Krishna describes the worshippers of the manifested God, thus,

महात्मानस्तु मां पार्थ दैवीं प्रकृतिमाश्रिताः।
भजन्त्यनन्यमनसो ज्ञात्वा भूतादिमव्ययम्॥ IX.13॥
सततं कीर्तयन्तो मां यतन्तश्च दृढव्रताः।
नमस्यन्तश्च मां भक्त्या नित्ययुक्ता उपासते॥ IX.14॥

" But high souls, having a Godlike nature worship Me with minds of exclusive attachment, knowing Me to be undecaying and the origin of all beings. Ever repeating My names, practicing with firm resolution, saluting Me with devotion, they worship Me with eternal constancy." At the end of the Gita, after the whole teaching is wound up Sri Krishna says "Hear again My greatest advice, the greatest of all secrets; since you are My sure devotee, I will tell your own good. Be minded in Me, you will reach Me alone, I assure you, as you are My dearest." (XVIII- 64, 65). The Gita therefore holds it of the utmost importance that the aspirant should take to the adoration of the personal God in the most reverent attitude possible. In this connection, we cannot resist the temptation of quoting another Gita text on the point with the commentary of Sri Sankaracharya, himself one of the staunchest advocates of Nirguna Brahman or Un-manifested God.

मत्कर्मकृन्मत्परमो मद्भक्तः सङ्गवर्जितः।
निर्वैरः सर्वभूतेषु यः स मामेति पाण्डव॥XI.55॥

"He who does my work, regards me as the highest, is without enmity towards all beings, he reaches me, Oh, Pandava." Sri S'ankaracharya introduces the s'loka in his commentary thus: " Now, the essential point of the whole scripture of the Gita, meant for salvation is here given out in a nut-shell for practice." Then the commentary runs thus: "Matkarmakriti, He who does My Work; Action for My sake is My work. Matparamah, the servant does the work of his master but never takes the master for the highest to be reached after his death, but this man does My work and considers Me the highest goal. Hence he is Matparamah (to whom I am the highest goal); so Madbhaktah, he worships Me by all means, in all forms and with all heart hence he is My Bhakta (devotee); Sangavarjitah without Sanga that is without fondness for and attachment to the enjoyments of wealth, Children, frineds, wife and relations. Nirvairassarvabhuteshu without enmity even towards those who are engaged in doing the greatest evil to him; he whoo is like this, he reaches Me. I and nothing else will be his destination. This is My teaching to you, Oh Pandava."

Spiritual relations resulting from Bhakti

To the Bhakta thus devoted realisation will become the easiest of things. Sri Krishna says elsewhere in the Gita

तेषां सततयुक्तानां भजतां प्रीतपिर्वकम् ।

ददामि बुद्धियोगं तं येन मामुपयान्ति ते ॥ X.10॥

तेषामेवानुकुम्पार्थमहमज्ञानजं तमः ।

नाशयाम्यात्मभावस्थो ज्ञानदीपने भास्वता ॥ X.11॥

"To them who are earnestly attached to Me, and worship Me with love, I give that direction of will by which they come to Me. Out of mercy to such alone, I seated in their heart destroy the darkness born of ignorance by means of a brilliant spiritual illumination." Thus it remains finally true that while the head knows the Lord, the heart it is which enters the innermost sanctuary and enjoys the sight of the Lord. Sri Krishna says

भक्त्या मामभिजानाति यावान्यश्चास्मि तत्त्वतः ।

ततो मां तत्त्वतो ज्ञात्वा विशते तदनन्तरम् ॥ XVIII.55॥

"Through Bhakti he recognises how great I am; actually knowing me though that Bhakti, he is assimilated into Me who am not far from him." This is the state of the devotee when Para Bhakti or supreme devotion is reached.

Human representation of Divine Love

It is indeed impossible to express in human language the burning love which the Bhakta feels for God. Just by way of suggestion, however human relations are given in comparison to the love. Thus Arjuna says, " You will please forgive me , Oh Lord, as a father would forgive his son, or a friend his companion, or a lover his beloved." Addressing God as father has been a universal practice among religions, but denotes the intensity to divine love; even an intimate friend's love has been thought insufficient by Bhaktas. Religious men have exhausted the list of human relations of love in representing God love. For, God has been represented not only as father, but also as mother, grand-father, friend, protector, Creator, King, guardian, teacher etc., as we can see from the Gita (IX – 17, 18, XI- 43).

These however are merely suggestions and can never exactly represent the intense love that Bhaktas feel for the Lord. Their state is thus described by Sri Krishna :

मच्चित्ता मद्गतप्राणा बोधयन्तः परस्परम्।
कथयन्तश्च मां नित्यं तुष्यन्ति च रमन्ति च ॥ X.9 ॥

"Even minded in Me, holding life for Me, teaching one another and ever relating My glory, they please themselves and make merry." Thus respect for the Lord, joy in His presence, misery in feeling separate from Him, distaste for worldly things, complete dependence on the Lord and perfect self-surrender are the chief characteristics of the Bhaktas. Out of the fullness of their hearts, they have frequently given expression to their feelings. They feel the presence of the beloved
God so near that they call him lord, mother, father, friend, nay more the Self. They feel and most confidently assert "I and my Lord are one." They are filled with God to such an extent that they would not like to hear of the slightest separation from Him. It is this view that Sri Krishna endorses when he says:

समोऽहं सर्वभूतेषु न मे द्वेष्योऽस्ति न प्रियः।
ये भजन्ति तु मां भक्त्या मयि ते तेषु चाप्यहम्॥ IX.29॥

" I am the same to all beings and there is no one hated or loved of Me; but as for them that worship Me with devotion they eternally live in Me, and I in them.

उदाराः सर्व एवैते ज्ञानी त्वात्मैव मे मतम्।
आस्थितः स हि युक्तात्मा मामेवानुत्तमां गतिम्॥ VII.18॥

" Again, Sri Krishna says elsewhere " The enlightened Bhakta is My very self (VII- 18)"

The ideal of Para Bhakti

When this supreme state of blessedness is reached, all forms and ceremonies become useless; promise or threat of Sastras loses its force alike; the misery due to the Gunas of Maya vanishes forever and in its lace comes eternal unbounded bliss. Such a Bhakta would say with the Gita,

नादत्ते कस्यचित्पापं न चैव सुकृतं विभुः।
अज्ञानेनावृतं ज्ञानं तेन मुह्यन्ति जन्तवः॥ V.15॥

"The Lord neither takes away voice nor accepts a meritorious action of any souls; true knowledge being covered up with ignorance, being befool themselves." It must not be concluded from this that the ideal Bhakta is reckless and willful in his ways, being quite unmindful of the Sastras. The s'loka just quoted only means that Bhakta has so far overcome all interested motives, that he does good not because of Sastric injunctions, not because he expects a reward or desires to escape some punishment, but because it has become a habit with him to do good. He has realised the maxim "It is only noble to be good." In discussion this point, the famous Sureswaracharya says "When the Atman is realised, will humbleness and other self-less activities vanish along with interested activities, (both being the result of ignorance) or will the former not disappear? We reply, they will not. What is the reason? Because the supreme Atman is of his own nature, unopposed to injunctions of self-less activities. But (this non-removal of good qualities is not because of the injunction. How else then? Listen; to the person in whose the realisation of the Atman has been born, non-hatred and other qualities (Cf. अद्वेष्टा सर्वभूतानां etc., XII- 13 to 19) will be a habit requiring no effort, but no longer will they be virtuous to be acquired by conscious action." (Naishkarmyasiddhi IV – 69). To such an ideal Bhakta with whom it has become a habit to do good, it is immaterial whether pleasure or pain falls to his lot, whether people accord him praise or blame. In spite of the changing external environment he remains forever undisturbed, because he has found the source of eternal bliss. He has realised that the ideal of love, the essence of all love is itself bliss. His unbounded love reveals to him the truth that the whole universe is one ocean of bliss. He sees that all beings are only waves great or small in that ocean. He has, in fact, understood the true meaning of the Upanishadic statement "

आनन्दो ब्रह्मेति व्यजानात् । आनन्दाध्येव खल्वमिानि
भूतानि जायन्ते । आनन्देन जातानि जीवन्ति ।
आनन्द प्रयन्त्यभसिंवशिन्तीति ।
सैषा भार्गवी वारुणी विद्या । परमे व्योमन्प्रतिष्ठिता ।
स य एवं वेद प्रतितिष्ठति । अन्नवानन्नादो भवति ।
महान्भवति प्रजया पशुभिर्ब्रह्मवर्चसेन । महान् कीर्त्या ॥

"From bliss only, indeed, are these beings born, being born they live in bliss, and it is bliss that they finally approach and are there into assimilated." And when one has identified oneself with this ocean of bliss, how can there be dissatisfaction or disturbance? This ideal person therefore may be said to have realised the true Yoga. For, what is Yoga? "Evenness is Yoga."

<u>The relation between Bhakti Yoga and Jnana Yoga</u>

In Para Bhakti , we have a point of convergency where both Jnana Yoga and Bhakti Yoga meet. Different though they might appear at first sight, the two Yogas are really closely inter-related as already shown, and at this stage they again mingle in one. When a Jnana Yogin attains that ripe condition of knowledge, called "Jnana Nishtha" or firm adherence to knowledge (XVIII – 50), his realization becomes absolutely indistinguishable from Para Bhakti. In fact Sri Krishna calls Jnanin his highest devotee (VII- 17) and when knowledge coupled with all its ripening aids and free from antagonistic influences develops into supreme realization of the Atman, it is called "Nishtha." And it is this Jnana Nishtha or fully developed Jnana that is identical with Para Bhakti. It is this Bhakti that Vaman Pandit the famous medieval Sadhu and poet of the Mahabharata so much extols in his commentary on the Bhagavadgita called "Yatahrtha Dipika." Thus while the preparatory Bhakti (Gouni Bhakti) leads to the knowledge of Brahman (Brahmajnanam) the supreme Bhakti (Para Bhakti) is the final consummation of Jnana generally known as Brahma Nishtha. This fact that Para Bhakti is the fulfillment of Jnana, accounts for the position accorded to Bhakti Yoga after Jnana Yoga in the present treatment.

[1] *The Religion of Jesus, p. 35, by the Rev. N. Macnicol.*
[2] *Swami Vivekananda*

CHAPTER FIVE

Renunciation

All rituals and customs meant for spiritual refinement are important for the spiritual ascent of the fellow aspirants, but such rituals can have some sort of limits. We will discuss few incidents from epics to reflect this proposition in detail.

Emperor Bali is generally addressed Bali Chakravatri[1]. He is the grandson of Prahlaada, who in turn is the son of greatest demon king, Hiranyakashyapa, who was eliminated by Vishnu, in His Nara-simha, Man-Lion incarnation. The fellow emperor conducted a very grand Vedic ritual. While remaining as its officiator all the gods personally approached Vishnu, keeping Fire-god ahead of them to request him to ensure completion of all the rituals meant for gods. Whoever the supplicant might be and from wherever the seeker might be approaching the emperor, but if one approaches and supplicates to the fellow king he is donating that in "as is where is condition", whatever is supplicated and wherever it might be. Appeal of gods to Vishnu was to check the progression of emperor Bali in the holy path of attainment of the highest status of donor in the context. It was the result of TAPA[2] (or meditation) with which emperor Bali wanted to ascend in the path of Spirituality; such kind of ascent was supplemented considerably by the extensive charity with which the fellow king wanted to proceed. Sage Kashyapa identified presence of entire universe in lord Vishnu; even he identified himself in the Divine; a concept of Vishwaroopa[3]. Sage Kashyapa and Aditi materialised origin of Bamana (the form of lord Vishnu) for checking the ceaseless advancement of emperor Bali. Sage Baman approached the place where emperor Bali was offering charity to seekers; it was the holy conduct with which the fellow emperor wanted to gain fame and familiarity; an act which would have been enough for gaining the status of godly characters; a conduct which would have been a suffice for claiming regulation of three realms of manifestation.

Description: C:\Users\Web Hosting\Pictures\12.jpg

"Sage Vaamana begged and received a space from emperor Bali that can be covered in three strides[4], but strode all the three worlds in those three steps for the purpose of saving the entire manifestation, as he is interested in the welfare of all the worldly manifestations. Lord Vishnu gave the earth back to Indra restraining Emperor Bali with his vitality."[5]

We all know that Alexander invaded India main land during the ancient age when Aryan group looing after different states of India main land were not united. The fellow Greek warrior succeeded by part and considered himself as victorious. Some of the princely states were not accessible to them because of many reasons. His men finally refused to fight and Alexander preferred returning back to his native place.

During one of instance when his men continued returning back some peculiar type of people were identified by them. Some of them remained engaged in preparing a yard of land to be used by them. They continued measuring that land by jumping side by side. Alexander wanted to know the exact reason because of which they were behaving in such a peculiar way. One of the saintly person admitted, "You came here to consider yourself as victorious. You want to grab all the lands. Then also you may not remain eligible for gaining ownership of all the lands. You will be entitled an access to merely a stretch of a yard of land, not more than that.'

After such conversation Alexander admitted that there are three types of people in this land: Some people work for gaining money and property, some other people work for earning fame; there is third type of people. Like these men, having no expectation from people or state. They simply work for the betterment of people without expecting anything in return. They also move through renunciation for making people and states competent and stronger. If somebody wants to rule this land then they have to win the confidence of these third types of people (Third Power).

Renunciation cannot be ascribed as any escape from delivering duty to society or to escape regular economic practices for the purpose of earning a living for the community. It is also not the state during which person start gaining some additional privileges from society. Renunciation is the subject beyond the scope of religious confinement. We can expect some sort of matured approach to social subjects through which prosperity and advancement of a society can be ensured.

Renunciation is a state of approach adopted by an individual by casting off the affinity towards gaining advantages in return to services provided to society. It also ensures an intellectual and spiritual advancement of an individual needed for actualising oneself in the situation during which such individual start searching out alternative ways through which prosperity of fellow members of a community can be ensured. India has a bright history of renunciation. People from different walks of life renunciated the world for gaining prosperity meant for commons. Examples are there in plenty.

A youth from a promising farmer's family from Punjab got an assignment to go to market for selling out some farm produces for earning a profit. While moving towards the market place they were moving through a poverty struck village. They preferred feeding fellow villagers by using farm produces that they were carrying to the market. Family members of the youth came to know about the incident and were not happy because of the act. Without considering the willingness of the family members the fellow youth preferred continuing his service to poor and hungry. He also started preaching people by introducing them with noble deeds and wiser conducts. In gradual succession he preferred renunciation for the purpose of continuing his service to humanity.

State of renunciation will come after attainment of true knowledge. The term true knowledge concerns with the understanding of an individual with which omnipresence of the divine in every creation can be visualized. With such apprehension that individual start delivering society without expecting anything in return. Renunciation can be considered as a kind of intellectual .spiritual and mental enlightenment of the individual leading the person ultimately towards a state of spiritual bliss, with which special attention towards collective progress of society can be advanced. Service oriented mission developed at different places in the world exhibits several examples of renunciation. Renunciation is still going on at different places at different instances with varying objectives to work out some sort of service lines meant for ensuring collective progress of desired types.

A youth from Kolkata prepared himself for renunciation after receiving spiritual instructions of divine Teacher. During one instance the youth observed that his master performs a special type of meditation. That meditation was of a special type because of which his fellow teacher was becoming capable of gaining an instant lift from the ground. The fellow youth approached his master and wanted to learn the special type of meditation. Master was not happy after learning about the affinity of the fellow w youth towards attainment of personal advancement. The fellow master said, "I thought you will become a banyan tree , but you are trying to become a palm tree! You are nothing but a Useless fellow!"

Attainment of personal advancement without considering immediate need of other people of society was not preferable by the divine master. He wanted the youth to work the progress of the entire community (collective progress). It was the way of renunciation which was preferred by Mahatma. Renunciation should be of such type which cannot imply additional burden upon society. It should have enough capability to address the issues and concerns of the adjoining society. Individual having such kinds of collective impetus can deliver services to needy and disadvantaged people. Renunciation having strict motive of individual progress is absolutely a non-desirable effort. Person who renunciated the world with such kind of restricted affinity of individual progress may not become that much effective in making the entire community that much prosperous. Third power can also have an impetus on the process of reviving human relations in a society. Saintly persons of such genre are the source of inspiration with which community segments often prefer getting involved in the process of revivals and reforms of desired types through the process of socialisation and acculturation.

Growth of spirituality went on progressive through two distinct paths: Advaita (non-duality) and Dvaita (duality).[6] Advaita emphasises practice of the Yoga of Knowledge in three distinct stages.[7] One should lead active, creative and practical life of truthfulness, fidelity, self-control and purity.[8] At certain instances the term "religion" is replaced by the term "Spirituality" to ensure expansion of the scope of spiritual ascent in modern society.[9] Further progress in this path is ascertained by accommodating scopes of human development, psychology and capacity building leading aspirants finally to realisation of the self.[10] At final instances of progress in addressing spirituality beyond the restricted scope of customs and religion brings the scope of making aspirants aware of the situation of experiencing deepest value and meanings of the soul by which regulation of senses can be materialised in day to day living.[11] Gaining spiritual experience through guided practices plays central role in modern society.[12] It has further influence on the mordernist streams of Asian traditions, making the process easily recognisable for aspirants of west.[13] Emphasis on gaining personal experience replaced the authority of scriptures.[14] It is also becoming equally relevant for people seeking tension free life and people encountering various types of psychological and physical disorders.[15] Spiritually oriented aspirants experience higher intrinsic meaning of life, eternal peace and strength; they also extend enhanced social support to community members.[16] Application of Yoga, Meditation and Spiritual practices contemplate medical – technical approaches to ensure improvement of treatments. There exists restrictions in terms of measurement of spiritual progress at different instances of ascent because of lack any kinds of development parameters of specific types; such development is actually ensured by the Divine master; such kinds of development may be of different types and of different degrees.[17]

[1] Bali, The Emperor, known for his grand benevolence; his courage and will power.

[2] The word 'tapaH'(Hindi word Tapasya) also means jnaana, gnosis, knowledge, intellect, spirit, will power, confidence factors, as such it is oriented that way; even lord Vishnu is abounding with intellect, aggregate of intellect, the only aspect of intellect, etc.

[3] The physique of universe which lord Krishna explained to Arjuna in The Bhagavadgita.

[4] Lord Vishnu is eulogised as Trivikrama, tri- vi-krama three, verily, paced - surpassing, one who surpasses all the three worlds in just three strides.

[5] Sri Valmiki Ramayana; Chapter 1

[6] Ramakrishna Puligandla (1985), Jñâna-Yoga – The Way of Knowledge (An Analytical Interpretation), University Press of America New York, ISBN 0-8191-4531-9;

Fort, A.O. (1998), Jīvanmukti in Transformation: Embodied Liberation in Advaita and Neo-Vedanta, State University of New York Press, ISBN 0-7914-3903-8;

Richard King (1999), Indian philosophy: An introduction to Hindu and Buddhist thought, Edinburgh University Press, ISBN 0-7486-0954-7, p. 223;

Sawai, Y. (1987), The Nature of Faith in the Śaṅkaran Vedānta Tradition, Numen, 34(1), pp. 18–44

[7] jñāna yoga in stages: samnyasa (cultivate virtues), sravana (hear, study), manana (reflect) and dhyana (nididhyasana, contemplate)

[8] Marwha, Sonali Bhatt (2006). Colors of Truth, Religion Self and Emotions. New Delhi: Concept Publishing Company. p. 205. ISBN 978-81-8069-268-0.

[9] *Gorsuch, R.L.; Miller, W.R. (1999), "Assessing spirituality", in W.R. Miller (ed.), Integrating spirituality into treatment, Washington, DC: American Psychological Association, pp. 47–64*

[10] *Lockwood, Renee D. (June 2012). "Pilgrimages to the Self: Exploring the Topography of Western Consumer Spirituality through 'the Journey'". Literature and Aesthetics. 22 (1): 108. Archived from the original on 12 October 2022. Retrieved 19 September 2019. The new Western spiritual landscape, characterised by consumerism and choice abundance, is scattered with novel religious manifestations based in psychology and the Human Potential Movement, each offering participants a pathway to the Self.*

[11] *Ewert Cousins, preface to Antoine Faivre and Jacob Needleman, Modern Esoteric Spirituality, Crossroad Publishing 1992.*

[12] *Sharf, Robert H. (1995), "Buddhist Modernism and the Rhetoric of Meditative Experience" (PDF), NUMEN, 42 (3): 228–283, doi:10.1163/1568527952598549, hdl:2027.42/43810, archived from the original (PDF) on 2019-04-12, retrieved 2013-02-10*

[13] *Sharf, Robert H. (1995), "Buddhist Modernism and the Rhetoric of Meditative Experience" (PDF), NUMEN, 42 (3): 228–283, doi:10.1163/1568527952598549, hdl:2027.42/43810, archived from the original (PDF) on 2019-04-12, retrieved 2013-02-10*

[14] *Sinari, Ramakant (2000), Advaita and Contemporary Indian Philosophy. In: Chattopadhyana (gen.ed.), "History of Science, Philosophy and Culture in Indian Civilization. Volume II Part 2: Advaita Vedanta", Delhi: Centre for Studies in Civilizations*

[15] *Joshanloo, Mohsen (4 December 2010). "Investigation of the Contribution of Spirituality and Religiousness to Hedonic and Eudaimonic Well-Being in Iranian Young Adults". Journal of Happiness Studies. 12 (6): 915–30. doi:10.1007/s10902-010-9236-4. S2CID 143848163.*

[16] *Salsman, J.M.; Brown, T.L.; Brechting, E.H.; Carlson, C.R. (2005). "The link between religion and spirituality and psychological adjustment: The mediating role of optimism and social support". Personality and Social Psychology Bulletin. 31 (4): 522–35. doi:10.1177/0146167204271563. PMID 15743986. S2CID 34780785.*

[17] *MacDonald, Douglas A.; Friedman, Harris L.; Brewczynski, Jacek; Holland, Daniel; Salagame, Kiran Kumar K.; Mohan, K. Krishna; Gubrij, Zuzana Ondriasova; Cheong, Hye Wook; Sueur, Cédric (3 March 2015). "Spirituality as a Scientific Construct: Testing Its Universality across Cultures and Languages". PLOS ONE. 10 (3): e0117701.*

Bibcode:2015PLoSO..1017701M.   doi:10.1371/journal.pone.0117701.   PMC 4348483. PMID 25734921.

Concluding Remarks

It now remains for us to briefly recapitulate what has been said in the preceding pages in order to enable ourselves to frame an answer to the question with which the present book began.

We have seen that the Bhagavadgita is a treatise on Brahmavidya and Yogas'astra and that Yoga is the one indispensable condition in which Brahma Vidya or the knowledge of Brahman is attained. That this is so borne out not only from the contents of the Gita in almost every chapter of which the knowledge of Brahman is spoken of, and the means of attaining it is set forth as Yoga, but also from the express statement "यत्र न चैवायन स्थितिश्चलति तत्वतः" (standing where one never swervs from the Truth). Here we are told directly that Yoga is that frame of mind in which one never loses sight of the Truth of Brahman.

It has also been seen that the Yoga intended as a means to Brahma Vidya is defined in the Gita itself as "equanimity." A good many commentaries both on ancient and modern lines have attempted to solve what this Yoga means and what the essence of the Gita is in their own way. Thus S'ankaracharya , whose commentary is the oldest available, says that Sri Krishna taught Arjuna the twofold Vedic religion, of works (Pravrittilakshan) and commentator Supreme Bliss of Moksha is attainable by Jnana Yoga. According to Ramanujacharya, the next commentator, the Gita intends to set forth the Bhakti Yoga supported by knowledge as well as works (ज्ञानकर्मानुगृहीतभक्तियोग). The system of Nimbarkacharya is slightly different from that of Ramanuja, but still it may be put down as recoognising Bhakti Yoga as the essence of the Gita. Madhavacharya also teaches Bhakti though according to him knowledge Buddhi Yoga is the primary meaning of "Yoga" and the essential condition of Moksha. According to Vallabhacharya who is a Vaishnava commentator like Ramanuja or Madhava, but the expounder of a modified Advaitism unlike either, the Gita expounds chiefly Bhakti as calculated to bring on Divine grace. In later times the famous Jnaneshwara of Maharashtra wrote a learned commentary in Marathi, on the Gita very much in accord with the views of S'ankara but specializing the importance of Bhakti. Of the modern writers, Dr. Thibaut though that Bhagvata system was chiefly represented in the Gita. Dr Sir R. G. Bhandarkar, according to whom the Gita represents a theistic reaction against antagonistic influence, passes over the definition of Yoga in the text and simply says "The condition of mind in the Yoga mode is a determined will." Though Pandit Sitanath Tattvabhushan of Calcutta refers to the Gita definition of Yoga in his book called "Krishna and Gita" (p.177), he does not seem to attach much importance to it, for he seem to be more or less identify it with Dhyana Yoga (p. 183, ibid), and later on with Bhakti, though he thinks the philosophy of the Gita is Bhedabhed Vada utterly opposed to Maya Vada, (p. 249, ibid). Prof. M. Rangacharya of Madras has recently published his class lectures on the Bhagavadgita in which he gives prominence to ethics as is evident from very name of the discussion "The Hindu Philosophy of Conduct." Mr. Bal Gangadhar Tilak of Poona thinks that Karma Yoga is the Yoga meant to be taught in the Gita and according to him that Jnanin ought to work for the good of the world is the central doctrine of the work. He accordingly styles the Gita as Karma-Yoga-Sastra. This scholar also has revived a controversy as to the true position of Karma in the Gita, besides adding a new tenet of his own, unlike all other commentators, that the Gita teaching is meant for Jnanins and not for aspirants only.

It is not necessary, however, for us to pursue here the enquiry as to the exact position of Karma in the Gita, for the real point at issue is what the Yoga of the real point at issue is what the Yoga of the Gita is and in the preceding pages we have shown that it is "equanimity" and that this definition applies equally to Karma, Dhyana, Jnana and Bhakti. Accordingly Sri Krishna says

उपद्रष्टाऽनुमन्ता च भर्ता भोक्ता महेश्वर:।

परमात्मेति चाप्युक्तो देहेऽस्मिन्पुरुष: पर:॥XIII .23॥

ध्यानेनात्मनि पश्यन्ति केचिदात्मानमात्मना।

अन्ये सांख्येन योगेन कर्मयोगेन चापरो॥ XIII 25॥

" By concentration some behold the self in the self by self, other by Sankhya Yoga, and others by Karma Yoga. Yet others, not knowing this, worship, having heard from others; they too cross beyond death, adhering to what they heard." Here Dhyana Yoga and Karma Yoga are recognised expressly by their own name, Jnana Yoga is also recognised by its alternative title Sankhya Yoga, for it has been stated t be expressly meant for Sankhyas in an earlier chapter (II – 3) . The word "worship" clearly refers to Bhakti coupled with faith. Thus all the four lead to the realisation of the Atman, that is, are the means to Brahma Vidya. Each of these four leadsw to "equanimity" the real Yoga, and thus helpful to the realization of Brahman. Hence there can be little doubt that the Gita as Yoga Sastra lays special stress on Yoga as equanimity. Some of the modern writers, however are disposed to think that Yoga has an alternative definition "योग: कर्मसु कौशलम्" and according to them this means "Skill in actions is called Yoga," but this view ignores the context altogether. The passage in which the verse occurs runs thus; -

योगस्थः कुरु कर्माणि सगं त्यक्त्वा धनंजय ।

सद्धियसद्धियो: समो भूत्वा समत्वं योग उच्यते ॥

दूरेण ह्यवरं कर्म बुद्धियोगाद्धनञ्जय।

बुद्धौ शरणमन्वच्छि कृपणा: फलहेतव:॥ II.49॥

बुद्धियुक्तो जहातीह उभे सुकृतदुष्कृते।

तस्माद्योगाय युज्यस्व योग: कर्मसु कौशलम्॥ II.50॥

' Steadfast in Yoga do they works, O, Dhananjaya, casting off attachment, being the same in success and failure. Equanimity is called Yoga. Far removed is lower Karma, from the Yoga of intelligent work; O wealth – winner, seek refuge in this wisdom, for pitiable are those that are led by desires of rewards. He, who is endowed with the wisdom leaves behind both the good and the bad, wherefore apply thyself to Yoga. In regard to actions, Yoga is the skill." Obviously Sri Krishna is here pointing to Arjuna, how actions should be performed in order that they may not be binding. He says that they must be performed with Yoga (or equanimity), without being perturbed in mind by success or failure; he then contrasts this sort of work with Yoga with selfish work and condemning the latter, praises the former as a great power, inasmuch as actions which are of a binding nature lose that nature when done with evenness of mind. Then karma Yoga is concluded with the word: "Therefore apply thyself to Yoga." Some have thought that BUDDHI in the last verse refers to knowledge as contrasted with work, apparently on the ground that it is only for the Jnanin that leaving both the good and the bad is possible. But the conclusion "Therefore apply yourself to Yoga" is a sufficient guarantee that Buddhi is really "Samatwabuddhi". Though it is true that actions are not binding on a jnanin, we may be sure that we are here concerned with the fruits of actions only, for the next verse says: "For men of wisdom caste off the fruit of action, possessed of knowledge, 9and) released from the bond of birth, they attain the state where there is no evil" (II- 51). In any case it must be more than clear that "equanimity" is the only Yoga thought of in the

Gita. We have shown in the preceding pages how all the four Yoga lead to this ideal Yoga and how as such they are not really so many distinct path, but are really inter-related. This explains why the Gita begins with Jnana and introduces Karma Yoga and finally concludes with Dhyana Yoga in one place, while it begins with Karma Yoga and treating of the other two Yogas concludes with the Jnana Yoga in another place. We may select here a passage in the last chapter of the Gita, where this inter-relation is more clearly suggested than elsewhere in the work. "Devoted each to his own duty, man attains perfection; how devoted to one's own duty one attains success, that do thou hear. Him from whom is the evolution of all beings, by whom all this is pervaded, by worshipping Him with his proper duty, man attains perfection (XVIII – 45-46). This shows how Karma Yoga and Bhakti Yoga are related, how actions performed as worship become a means of perfection. Again "He whose mind is free from attachment everywhere, whose self is subdued, from whom desire has fled, he by renunciation attains that supreme state of freedom from action." (XVIII – 49). Here is indicated the relation between Karma Yoga and Jnana Yoga, how actlessness of the self is realised through unselfish work. Take these verses now. "Endowed with a pure mind, controlling the self with firmness, leaving aside objects like sound, giving up love and hatred, resorting to a sequestered spot, eating but little, speech and body and mind subdued, always engaged in meditation and concentration, taking refuge in dispassion, having abandoned egotism, strength, arrogance, desire, enmity, property, free from the notion of mind and peaceful, he becomes fit for becoming Brahman." (XVIII- 51 -53). We are told in these s'lokas how Dhyana Yoga leads to Brahma Vidya or realisation of Brahman. Thus it is quite possible to conceive of how Karma Yoga necessarily involves Bhakti Yoga, Jnana Yoga and through Dhyana Yoga leads to realisation of the Brahman. And we might quote other similar passages to establish similar sequences of Yoga in a different order. This should be enough, therefore to show not only that the Gita does not consider the Yogas as mutually exclusive, but also that it implies the necessity of a certain order of discipline to be followed.. But still the fact remains, that according to the temperament of religious aspirant he would be called a Yogin in accordance with the method preferred by him.

It is this peculiarity of the Gita that has baffled many a commentator, who started with a preconceived theory that the Gita wanted to establish a particular Yoga as supreme. As it is not the purpose of the present attempt to critically examine any of these theories, we may simply repeat here again the observation made in the introductory remarks that none of these exclusive theories can find any support in the Gita. According to the Gita, we may repeat, the ideal Yoga is equanimity and whatever leads up to that Yoga is itself a Yoga.

It is now time to formulate an answer to the main question with which we started the present discussion. "What is the value of the Gita as a guide to practical life?" If by practically we mean a teaching to be reconciled to our present life which merely sanctions the way in which we live in the world, however gross may be its defects, then the Gita, to be plain, is absolutely of no value as a guide. For, the teachings are antagonistic to most of our conceptions of life. People of the ordinary frame of mind are, it is to be feared, mostly opposed in their trend of thought to the doctrines of the Gita. They believe in competition, in the theory that might is right, that the pleasurable is necessarily the eternal destiny of mankind and that one's interest is identical with one's duty. If this be the practical life, it may be confessed at once, the Gita is at best indifferent to it, but is certainly no guide to those that wish to lead such a life. But there is another kind of practical life. Instead of trying to reconcile the ideal with our present life, we might try to gradually improve ourselves till we approach the ideal. This ideal, however high it may be, must not be an impossible one. In this sense the ideal of the Gita is quite practical. Brahma- Vidya is its ideal, the realisation that Brahman or the Absolute is the self of us all. As observed elsewhere in the course of our discussion, everyone is consciously or unconsciously striving to attain the Highest Truth or Brahman. Owing to our not having an exact conception of what this ideal is are caused the different courses of action we take towards the realisation of it. Every man is therefore really following the path of Brahman, whatever course of conduct he may have chosen for himself and he is in the long run destined to take up deliberately the path of Brahman (IV- 11). Hence the realisation of Brahman becomes the ultimate goal of every one of us. Yoga or perfect equanimity is the one condition of actualising it. It goes without saying, therefore, that the teachings of the Gita offer the surest foundation for morality. While moral principles are only recommended in other sacred books without offering any philosophical basis for the same, the Gita is not only pre-eminently ethical in its nature, but supports it on the surest foundation of Brahma Vidya. We have had already occasion to note this in connection with Jnana Yoga . And it is this feature of the Vedatnta that has been specially appreciated by foreign admirers like Dr. Paul Deussen.

This scholar says " People have often reproached the Vedanta with being defective in moral and indeed the Indian genius is too contemplative to speak much of works, but the fact is, nevertheless, that the highest and purest morality is the immediate consequence of the Vedanta. The Gospel fix quite correctly as the highest law of morality : Love your neighbour as yourselves." But why should I do so, since by the order of nature I feel pain and pleasure only in myself, not in my neighbour. The answer is not in the Bible (this venerable book being not yet quite free of Semitic realism) but it is in the Vedas, is in the great formula "तत्वमसि (Tat twam asi)," which gives in three words metaphysics and moral together. You shall love your neighbour, as yourselves because you are your neighbour and mere illusion makes you believe that your neighbour is something different from yourselves. Or in the words of the Bhagavadgita, he who knows himself in everything and everything in himself will not injure himself by himself "Na hinasti atmana atmanam." This is the sum and tenour of all morality and this is the standpoint of a man knowing himself as Brahman"

If we remember the circumstances that led to the teaching of the Gita, how Arjuna, a fighting king, was taught things by Sri Krishna also a Kshatriya, in a battlefield, and how Arjuna is exhorted at every stage not to neglect his duty and how at the same time the highest philosophical truths are taught him as the one penance for all evils of this world, we can measure he extent of practicality of the philosophy and religion of the Gita. According to the Gita there are not two worlds- one of practical life and another of religious life, but there is one undivided life, and the truths of philosophy and religion are to be felt and realized here or nowhere. Accordingly it says

इहैव तैर्जति: सर्गो येषां साम्ये स्थितिं मनः।

नर्दोषं हि समं ब्रह्म तस्मादब्रह्मणि ते स्थिताः॥ V.19॥

" Even in this life is nature conquered by those whose mind rests on evenness." This verse occurring as it does after another which declares that "the wise see the same in a Brahmin endowed with wisdom and humility, in a cow, in an elephant, as also in a dog and in a dog-eating outcast." Clearly points out the practical nature of the Yoga of equanimity. This Yoga of equanimity is not to be attained by taking refuge in a jungle from the vicissitudes of life and doing nothing useful, it needs, no doubt, speaking from the standpoint of Dhyana Yoga, retirement into solitude not with an aimless discontentment, but with the express object of investigating the most important problems of life. Then again after the realization the ideal wise man is described throughout as in the above verses as spending his life in the very midst of the world. Whether they come in contact with the spirituality regenerated or with the worldly minded or even with the purely Tamasic souls who are not yet sufficiently developed to be fit for the busy concerns of life, they see in all the one and the same pure Brahman. Their very presence inspires other less- gifted souls, and their living personality is no small help to those that wish to keep up their balance of mind but are constantly tossed up and down by the waves of worldly life. Here is a very practical ideal, for every one of the thoughtful people on earth wants to get at a method whereby he can improve himself and be of some use to society. The Gita says to achieve this you must gain tranquility of mind, perfect balance of mind. Avoiding the extremes of inactivity अकर्म (Akarma) and activity with passion विकर्म (Vikarma), we should ever strive after intense activity, but in the midst of it, eternal calmness. Try to see the same Brahman in all, have before your mind constantly those great souls who are ever inspired with the Divine Atman, full of the Divine Atman and Atman alone (V- 17), and who see the same Divine Atman everywhere in this world of variety (V – 18), and you will have a great help to secure this calm, forgiving, equable, all-loving mind which is the condition of success in life.

And this practice does not require any extra ordinary special qualifications reserved only for a few. For Sri Krishna says

इदं ते नातपस्काय नाभक्ताय कदाचन।

न चाशुश्रूषवे वाच्यं न च मां योऽभ्यसूयति॥ XVIII.67॥

"This is not to be taught to one who is devoid of austerities; never to one who is not devoted; nor should it be taught to one who is not obedient, nor yet to one who is jealous of Me." These are the only conditions. On must undergo training of thought, word and deed. What this training is, is explained in the seventeenth chapter, "Worship purity, straightforwardness, continence and abstinenece from injury, speech which causes no excitement and is true, pleasant and beneficial, reading of the scriptures, serenity of mind, good-heartedness, silence, self-control and purity of nature" (XVII- 14 to 16). Practice of these constitutes Tapas. He must be devoted to God and willing to obey the injunctions. In a word, no special qualification is demanded except a sincere wish to improve oneself. Provided with this qualification one may practice the discipline from where he is placed by nature.

स्वे स्वे कर्मण्यभरितः संसिद्धिं लिभते नरः।

स्वकर्मनरितः सिद्धिं यथा वन्दिति तच्छृणु॥ XVIII .45॥

"Engaged in his own duty man attains perfection."

Thus the Gita is one of the highest practical value to those who wish to get over difficulties in this life- difficulties which are the results of wickedness and evil,- and to those who wish to improve themselves as well as their environment. We might with perhaps even more propriety quote the very expressions which have been applied to European mysticism and say "its teachings hold just as good in the family, in the market, in the Senate, in the study, aye in the battlefield itself, and teach (man) the way to lead in whatever station of life he may be placed a truly man like because a truly God –like life."